FORGED IN BATTLE

FORGED in BATTLE

AFRICAN AMERICAN OFFICERS SERVING IN THE UNITED STATES ARMY

CLEOLA M. DAVIS

NEW DEGREE PRESS

COPYRIGHT © 2022 CLEOLA M. DAVIS

All rights reserved.

FORGED IN BATTLE

African American Officers Serving in the United States Army

ISBN   979-8-88504-983-2   *Paperback*
              979-8-88504-984-9   *Kindle Ebook*
              979-8-88504-985-6   *Ebook*

dedication

In loving memory of my parents,
Mr. Edgar W. Davis and Mrs. Sarah Bell Neal Davis,

and to my paternal and maternal grandparents.

To my sister, Sarah Davis-Walker, and her family
Jerry, Jabari, Malik, and Courtney.

To all my cousins who have given love and support.

To my friend and great American hero Colonel (retired)
James M. Jones, and his wife Mrs. Jean Jones.

To the officers and soldiers of my company who carried
me through the lowest point of my life. Thank you.

In memory of the soldiers in my company
who died serving their country.

And honoring the African Methodist
Episcopal Church.

CONTENTS

AUTHOR'S NOTE

My memoir *"Forged in Battle: African American Officers Serving in the United States Army,"* chronicles true events as they occurred during the military service of two American Soldiers.

The book follows the ups and downs of my career in the military spanning over twenty years as well as shared stories with Vietnam War veteran and war hero Colonel (retired) James M. Jones. The memoir begins with Colonel Jones's story—a powerful story of strength and gallantry of a young second lieutenant exhibiting heroism usually only seen in movies.

My memoir was sparked on May 26, 2020, after witnessing the televised death of Mr. George Floyd. His helplessness while suffocating under the weight of a civil authority figure invoked trauma and stress I suppressed during and after my military service. Disturbed by my feelings, I reached out to a friend—Colonel (retired) Jones—who began telling me of an unresolved experience he had in 1967 while serving as a second lieutenant in Vietnam. As he talked, I began writing his story, and after a few sessions with him I began sharing and writing my stories. Together our experiences are merged to form *Forged in Battle*.

My experiences are told from my perspective, a woman's perspective as I mature during my journey from a naïve middle-class debutante to becoming among the first women in the United States Army to command a line unit in an Army armor division while in combat.

Through my experiences, I give voice to the voiceless people who survive their day-to-day jobs afraid to speak the truth of their situation. I am speaking for them. I am speaking for you.

Forged in Battle is action packed, thought provoking, and heartbreaking. No one has ever told a complex military war story like … *Forged in Battle*. It is both a soldier's story (one of gallantry, courage, honor, valor, and service); and one of fearless civil warriors facing and fighting multiple enemies in battles between right and wrong, friendships and enemies, black and white, leadership and cowardice, but above all faith and perseverance.

CHAPTER 1

GALLANT UNDER FIRE

Second Lieutenant James Jones, Platoon Leader, Charlie,
Company 1/327 Battalion, 1st Brigade (Separate) 101st Airborne
Division, in Vietnam, Fall 1967.

Witnessing the murder of Mr. George Floyd on television in May 2020, triggered symptoms akin to posttraumatic stress syndrome. I cried as life was squeezed out of his body while he lay helplessly. I have felt alone and helpless as the weight of American racism was holding me down while I suffocated. Unlike Mr. Floyd, I am alive to tell a true story, and I am compelled to do it because I am the only person who can. So many stories of the African American experience are untold, feeding the lie that we are happy with society as it exists. I believe this story will point out issues that should be fixed.

Sharing my thoughts about Mr. Floyd with my friend Colonel (retired) James M. Jones brought back memories of an incidents in his career that remains unresolved. Mr. Jones began to reflect …

***

I was a newly married second lieutenant just out of Airborne Jump school when I received orders to Vietnam. My assignment was third platoon Leader, Charlie Company, 1/327 Battalion, 1st Brigade (Separate) 101 Airborne Division. The company was nicknamed the "Cutthroats."

I arrived in the country on August 8, 1967; ten days after my platoon had suffered disastrous losses of half its members. The lieutenant who preceded me was among those killed. Most of the soldiers in my platoon were traumatized; suffering from the recent firefight and from a devastating fight they experienced in May. Most of them had lost confidence. Some of my men had seen two of their platoon leaders die; so, to them I was likely next. My first task was to build trust and morale because confronting the enemy was routine.

Existing soldiers had a close bond, but I had to integrate incoming replacement soldiers to form a team. Within my first few days I met with each soldier individually. Some of them were afraid and not ashamed of it. I prayed my favorite Bible verse, the twenty-third Psalm; some drew comfort from it, and some were moved to tears while reciting it with me. I requested and got the Chaplain to hold a service with the platoon as a group. During our session everyone was given the time to express their grief and share lessons learned from their tragedy.

It took every minute to train third platoon to have trust in each other even when assigned to defend our sector within the Firebase, where we lived. Every soldier slept, ate, and lived inside a fighting position guarding our sector. My platoon had between twenty-five and thirty members; numbers fluctuated due to the numbers of casualties and replacement changes. The platoon consisted of two radio telephone operators, two M-60 caliber machine gunners, two assistant gunners, two grenadiers, and a medic. The remaining soldiers were riflemen. I formed a special team I called the "Killer Team," consisting of a radio telephone operator, machine gunner, assistant gunner, grenadier, two riflemen, and me. My platoon sergeant oversaw the platoon whenever the Killer Team deployed. Within a week, trust and respect for me had grown significantly.

Heat, humidity, and the thick smell of jet fuel filled my nostrils. Heavy vegetation, trees, and brush abut areas cleared by engineers to provide clear lines of sight from the berm into defense sectors. The Firebase was a heavily engineered fortified command area. Constantia (barred) wire and sandbags provided levels of defense. A landing area for our transportation, the Utility Helicopter-1 Huey helicopter—the Learjet of the Infantry—was just outside the Firebase.

The Charlie Company commander divided the company in pairs of two platoons to maximize capability to accomplish multiple concurrent missions. My platoon, third platoon, was paired with fourth platoon which was led by First Lieutenant Castor. The first and second platoons were paired. Each individual platoon had a separate operating sector and separate areas to clear. Communication was by FM radio using our command frequency.

The evening of September 18, I received my platoon's next mission. The company sector was defined on a map, with separate sectors for each platoon. My platoon's sector had foliage and trails. Lieutenant Castor and fourth platoon were in the sector left of my platoon. Within his sector was a small village which he had to clear. The other two platoons were in sectors on Castor's left and our company command post element was following closely behind the platoons. Our combat assault mission was to search and destroy, sweeping everything within our sector. Search and destroy means find and kill the enemy.

I briefed my men … and asked if they had questions. I assured them we were ready and the mission was routine. Before departing we recited together the twenty-third Psalm as written in the King James Version of the Bible.

"The Lord is my shepherd; I shall not want. He maketh me to lie down in green pastures: he leadeth me beside the still waters.

He restoreth my soul: he leadeth me down the paths of righteousness for his name's sake.

Yea, though I walk through the valley of the shadow of death, I will fear no evil: for thou art with me; thy rod and thy staff they comfort me.

Early the next morning I heard the whirling sound of helicopter blades and felt their gushing wind as the company loaded on board our helicopters.

My mission was marked on my map; our designated landing zone was miles away, a clearing in the jungle where we started. At landing, the platoon disembarked the helicopter establishing security until the aircraft lifted off and out of sight. The landing zone was cold, meaning no enemy contact. Standing, I motioned to start the mission.

My platoon started moving down a path staggered to the left and the right of the trail about six feet apart heading toward our first objective, a point on the ground we would need to reach before moving to a new objective.

We were moving at a steady pace when suddenly, in the distance, I heard the popping sounds of AK-47s and the rattling of automatic weapons fire emanating from Lieutenant Castor's sector. I halted my platoon in place, anticipating orders from our company commander; silence, nothing.

Lieutenant Castor broke radio silence by calling the company commander for help. "Cutthroat, Cutthroat, this is Cutthroat forty … Taking heavy enemy fire, *over* … They are kicking the shit out of us … send help … we are laying out in the open; *over!*"

Cutthroat was the company commander's call sign. I didn't hear a response. A few seconds passed … I still didn't hear a response. Fourth platoon had walked into an ambush about fifty yards from the village made of one or two communal structures, four or five huts, and a dirt road; surrounded by trees, bush, and rice paddy fields.

From well concealed and fortified positions, North Vietnamese Army forces fired a heavy barrage of machine gun and automatic weapons nonstop. Castor's platoon was receiving heavy fires. Some soldiers were hit, and the entire platoon was pinned down in a rice patty.

Castor was screaming for help from the commander ..." I need some help ... they are shooting the shit out of us. I need someone to get here now! Send some freaking help before we are all killed ... supporting fires, over!"

Time seemed to stop ... I signaled for members of my Killer Team. "You, you, and you come with me." I have my 45mm pistol and my M1 Carbine rifle on me.

I yelled to my platoon sergeant, "Standfast with the rest of the guys until I call for you."

Within seconds me and the Killer Team were running toward the sound of gun fire. Before losing sight about fifty yards away, I signaled the Platoon forward.

From my position, I could see Lieutenant Castor who was still screaming calls for help from the command post.

At about fifty yards the Killer Team engaged the enemy. They took positions laying down suppressive fires on the enemy's left flank.

Lieutenant Castor's platoon was pinned down and spread out over about fifty yards of open ground. His soldiers were firing from behind small rice patty dikes to their front.

Lieutenant Castor was still screaming for help, "We are pinned down and taking casualties!"

North Vietnam forces were now engaging both our platoons; gun fire and the pound of mortar firings sounded throughout.

The platoon sergeant and other members of third platoon caught up and took positions reinforcing the Killer Team.

My soldiers had some cover inside the brush and jungle line. The terrain ahead was flat and open offering no protective cover and concealment except for berms four to five inches in height. Spotting the enemy in the tree line about fifty yards to our front, I positioned the gunners maximizing their suppressive fires on the enemy's flank.

Lieutenant Castor and the fourth platoon were positioned where the enemy could have surrounded them; I understood his frantic calls. The sound of gunfire, men yelling, and calls of "Medic, help medic!" created a dynamic urgent situation.

Vicious hails of murderous fires were falling on the exposed platoon's position. The situation was brutal. I just couldn't let Castor and his soldiers die in that firefight. I immediately deployed my troops and moved them forward to positions where they could place suppressive fire to relieve the pressure on Castor's men. I told my platoon sergeant to hold my platoon in position.

Although the enemy fire was intense, I believed I could make it to Castor who was totally pinned down, exposed, and still pleading for help. Without another thought, I ran to his position, I fell down next to him, and asked, "Are you OK, man?"

Lieutenant Castor was relieved to see me. "Damn man where did you come from?"

I said, "I heard you on the radio … and came to help. My guys are firing on your right … over there. You are going to be alright."

Lieutenant Castor responded, "Oh shit … thank you!"

Castor and I called for indirect supporting fires which was routine after a firefight. The enemy fled leaving behind their wounded, dead, and some weapons. Lieutenant Castor's platoon sustained casualties; medical support was called to evacuate them. No one in my platoon was wounded. After what seemed like a few minutes, I regrouped with my platoon, and we continued our mission in our sector.

The night was dark in the jungle. My platoon secured itself behind our claymore mines and in temporary foxholes and fighting positions. During my usual routine, I visit to each four-man fighting position. We went over some of the actions of the day. My soldiers insisted on giving me all the glory, but I emphasized our effectiveness as a team. As I moved about, I overheard some of my men describing my actions as fearless, brave, like a ferocious lion, unreal, like an Olympian running the fifty-yard dash. They celebrated how we kicked ass and saved Castor's platoon. I thank God.

After a while I told them, "Knock off the bull-shit, and get some sleep because we don't know what tomorrow may bring."

One soldier yelled out, "Hell yeah, today I killed as many as I could for my friends who died in our last firefight. I hate those bastards."

***

Mr. Jones stopped talking.

I was quiet too. I have read stories like this in books, and I've seen actors reenact this kind of gallantry in movies, but Mr. Jones was the first real man to tell me of a powerful experience such as this, that he lived through during combat. He makes me proud to be a veteran.

"Mr. Jones, after hearing this story I am humbled. You are a great man. I can't believe you didn't mention this during our twelve years of talking. I am very honored to know you, sir."

I see a different man. Mr. Jones's quiet, reserved, and dignified demeanor is now matched by his strength and gallantry in combat. He was fearless; a warrior, a man of action … a phenomenon.

Mr. Jones said, but how about this, "Months later after returning home I received a package in the mail containing a Bronze Star medal with valor device for that incident. I was both surprised and happy to be recognized, after all I was a lieutenant, and no one had said anything to me about the incident. To me it was just another day's work; a lot of other things happened after that incident, so I had forgotten about it.

"A few months after that, at my Infantry Advance Course, some fellow officers and I were remembering our time in Vietnam. One of them started naming the officers from our unit who received the Silver Star; I was surprised to hear Lieutenant Castor's name as a recipient.

Castor and I had kept in contact after leaving Vietnam, so I asked him, if it was true, that he got a Silver Star. He said he got one, and the only incident he had was the one in which I provided him aid."

Interrupting again, I asked Mr. Jones, "Are you saying they gave Castor the higher award? Please tell me no! Do you know why you were given the less prestigious award; an award lower than the one given the man you rescued?"

"No, I never understood that, but all indications are that either something was wrong or someone made a mistake. Now understand Ms. Davis, I have earned many awards, I have two Legends of Merit, but this award remains unre-solved because what was done appears wrong or should I say unjust and unexplained."

"Yes, I understand Mr. Jones, it seems something you earned was denied to you and given to someone else. According to Army Regulations 600-8-22 the Silver Star is awarded for gallantry; you were gallant and valorous under fire. Not to take anything from Lieutenant Castor, but if he deserved a Silver Star you certainly did. You were not required to place yourself in danger to help him, that act alone was above and beyond your duty. Was race the only difference between you and Castor? You are Black and he is White. If that was the reason, this is disgraceful."

"Well Ms. Davis, I have tried not to think of it in that way but what I've told you are the facts written in my award citation. Would you like to see my award citation? I will send it to you. You can draw your own conclusion. Castor and I were in the same unit, in the same position, leading about the same number of men, in the same war, with the same chain of command. You get my point."

"Yes Sir, I do. I would like to read your citation but more importantly I would like for you to receive the award you deserve."

"Well, Ms. Davis I don't think anything can be done about it. The regulation gives discretion in these matters to the commander. The honor and integrity of my commander is what this is about."

The Army is a microcosm of this country. As much as we want to believe the military has higher standards, nothing stops the Army from reflecting American society.

"You know Mr. Jones; I identify with having something taken from you for no reason other than race. So much happened to me during my time in service that I don't try to deny racism is deeply embedded in the fiber of the Army. The civil rights movement didn't do much to change the institutional norms in the Army that perpetuate racial discrimination. I battled to survive day-to-day from assignment to assignment. I prayed my way through the indiscriminate hatred, cruelty, and abuse. Yes sir, I have endured much, but I have persevered.

I entered the Army as a second lieutenant in 1983, about five years after the deactivation of the Army Women's Corps. That is important because I trained with male officers and didn't know anything different. But for some of the officers, Black women in positions of leadership in my branch, ordnance, and the other logistic specialties was new and unwelcomed.

"Ms. Davis, why do you say Black women? Why not all women?"

"I don't have any idea what it was like to be any color other than Black in the Army Mr. Jones; and look at what happened to you—a male. I had numerous challenges from the start—you know—being ignored and denied positions of higher responsibility. The best thing that happened was my assignment to division in Korea. Conditions there were about perfect because the mission focus overshadowed a lot of the pettiness associated with discrimination, and it gave me the opportunity to learn my trade while making good friends and growing spiritually. I left my first assignments in Corps at Fort Hood a first lieutenant, ordnance officer but departed the division in Korea a logistician. I knew maintenance operations, warehousing, basic air and ground transportation tracking, and so much more.

After completing my Advance Course, I returned to Fort Hood a captain—fired up and ready to command a company.

Mr. Jones, let me tell you, my story."

CHAPTER 2

CHEEKBONES HIGH

Corps Organization and Command Structure*		
Size	Organization	Officer Ranks
2 OR MORE DIVISIONS	CORPS	3-STAR GENERAL
3 OR MORE BRIGADES	DIVISION	2-STAR GENERAL
2 TO 5 BATTALIONS	BRIGADE/DISCOM	COLONEL
4 TO 6 COMPANIES	BATTALION	LIEUTENANT COLONEL
4 OR MORE PLATOONS	COMPANY	CAPTAIN
16-40 SOLDIERS	PLATOON	LIEUTENANT

Officer Ranks and Command structure in an Army Corps in 1990.
**Graphic created by author with input from Powers,*
Rod "How the US Army Is Organized," US Military Careers,
Military Branches. Updated on April 26, 2019.
How the US Army Is Organized (thebalancecareers.com)

"Davis, what did you do to the general? This morning in staff meeting the division commander told the DISCOM commander to put you in command and make sure it is a line company, not a headquarters," Colonel Scott Gibbs, commander of an armor brigade was talking to me on the phone.

I could hardly hold the phone in my hand. Even though I worked on his staff, I didn't know the general. I mean I had never talked with him or shared my plans with him. I thought I was just another captain to him; a division has hundreds of captains.

Colonel Gibbs continued, "The division commander, spoke very highly of your performance at the National Training Center in California, and he said when you briefed him in the field here you gave the best tactical briefing he had ever received from a logistics officer. He said you are talented Davis, good job."

I was so happy; I clapped my hands and did a little dance in excitement.

Colonel Gibbs emphasized how unusual it was for a two-star combat arms general to give a logistician an accolade of that kind. What a proud day for me. I studied hard to learn as much as I could about field operations, and my focus had paid off.

***

"Company," the first sergeant yells.
The platoon sergeants echo, "Platoon."
"Attention!"
The unit comes to attention.
September 25, 1989, was a beautiful, sunny day. In formation, the soldiers wore Kevlar helmets and pistol belts blending with the environment of perfectly groomed green grass. This was the day I had been waiting for; the day that I would take company command.

My face didn't show it, but my heart was beaming with happiness. At long last I was about to become a commander in a division at Fort Hood, Texas.

It had been a long journey to get here, and I didn't get here by myself. My mother was seated in the shade to my right looking beautiful wearing a hat and gloves. She traveled from North Carolina, representing my family; my father was ill and couldn't travel. She had pinned me second lieutenant at my commissioning ceremony when I graduated from North Carolina A & T State University. Yes, I have come a long way.

"At Close Interval, Dress Right Dress," the first sergeant's command disrupted my daydreaming.

"Ready, Front" the company snapped to attention.

I interviewed for this command over eighteen months before I first arrived at Fort Hood, but Captain Kinnear was given the position. I heard a senior logistics officer in Fort Hood, a one-star general recommended him. So, I had to wait and work to prove myself worthy of command; and I did.

The rumor among other logistics officers was Kinnear received an officer evaluation report stating he is "general officer material." Wow, now that says it all—general officer material? Kinnear and I are the same rank and joined the Army in the same year. I remembered him from a past assignment.

"Parade."

"Parade," platoon sergeants echo.

"Rest."

The ceremony was starting! I was so happy. This wonderful moment culminated years of hard work, training both in this division and the division in Korea. I was thankful and gave God praise.

The assumption of command ceremony is a simple ritual, passing the company guidon from the outgoing commander to the battalion commander, to me, followed by our speeches. After a reception at the officer's club, it was time to get to work.

I had a large maintenance company that repaired every type of equipment in the division's inventory except missile, aviation, and some high-ended communications and contracted equipment. The company—authorized about 200 people including myself, three lieutenants, and five chief warrant officers—was largest in the division.

I started by building strong relationships with my first sergeant and noncommissioned officers; no unit can be successful without them. I met each soldier during my pre-change of command property inventory that took place the thirty days leading to the ceremony, so I knew a little about everyone.

Every new job has challenges but before I could move into my office, I had some immediate problems.

Very little in my company was up to my standard. Excess property took up space in vehicle maintenance bays that were needed to conduct our mission which was equipment maintenance; other items were stuffed away inside storage containers. The maintenance tool room was unorganized and stored as much excess property as was authorized.

The first sergeant was marginal. The barracks were not highly maintained, soldiers didn't make company formations, the Orderly Room was messy, soldiers were not physically fit. After about forty-five days he moved to a position on the battalion staff, and I got a new, awesome first sergeant who had the strong leadership skills the company needed.

Getting the company positioned to progress toward meeting Army standards took about sixty days. During that time, I was aggravated by a few unexpected circumstances that astonished me as a new commander.

First, one of my lieutenants refused to follow my instructions. I wanted the best for my lieutenants; training them is one of my responsibilities, so I gave it priority.

I held meetings with my lieutenants who are commissioned officers, separately so I could assign tasks unique to their career paths—which was also my career path—and develop their skills.

As I walked through the maintenance work area shops one day, I noticed a task assigned to a lieutenant was undone and he was sitting at his desk in the maintenance office he shared with Chief Warrant Officer Porter. When I asked why the work wasn't done, the lieutenant stated he wasn't going to do it because the task was stupid. I didn't take time to counsel the lieutenant because refusing an order is unusual and unlawful. I believed the lieutenant had been emboldened to ignore my directives. I've heard rumors that this lieutenant and warrant officer attended meetings with my battalion commander, my predecessor Captain Kinnear, and my past first sergeant to discuss me and changes occurring in the company. Perhaps the second lieutenant, who was new to the Army, was confused by things he heard in those meetings. Not that I care that my battalion commander, my predecessor, and my officers were friends, but their personal relationships should not interfere with my command authority. I told the lieutenant to meet me in my office in ten minutes; I drove to the battalion commander's office to have the lieutenant, not the warrant officer, removed. I explained separating the two of them would give the lieutenant a fresh start and save his career. After explaining to the lieutenant why he was reassigned I never saw him again.

Next, one of my sergeants asked me for help. In my first company meeting, I announced my open-door policy; anyone could talk to me upon request if they informed their chain of command. After about ten days on the job as a female soldier, Staff Sergeant Christy asked to speak with me after duty hours. She explained the contents of our conversation were personal, asking to meet in her work area to ensure privacy. As requested, I arrived at her maintenance shop after duty hours. She was alone, standing at attention when I walked into her office. I asked that we sit and relax. She started to talk about her husband, who was accused of rape. She wanted my help because she was sure he didn't rape his accuser. I listened as she talked in circles, to share details about her life with her husband and the alleged rape.

I asked, "How do you know he didn't rape the girl?"

Staff Sergeant Christy said, "I don't think I can tell you, but believe me Ma'am I know he didn't do it. He is just not that kind of person."

I didn't see how I could help her based on what she had said.

She spoke slowly, "Well Ma'am, I just know he didn't do it … I know it because … he is gay, and so am I."

I was caught off guard.

Thinking quickly, "Stop. Before you say anything else. Let me read you your rights." I pulled a card out of my left breast pocket and mirandized her … "You have the right to remain silent. Anything you say can and will be used against you …"

I read it all as she sat looking at me.

Then I said, "Staff Sergeant Christy, I don't know why you decided to tell me this. Why you would jeopardize both yourself and your husband, but you have."

I was a little uneasy as she started to talk, "But Ma'am you said we could talk with you about anything."

She certainly was not going to test my integrity. I would not allow that. She wanted a response from me, and she got it.

Again she said, "I thought I could trust you with this … you said anything. We could talk about … anything."

I replied calmly, "Yes, you are right. I did … but our talk is now over."

I stood up, walked to the door, and paused, "The first sergeant will contact you about this matter." She stood to attention as I walked out the door.

This was certainly new to me. Everybody knew homosexuality was against Army policy and punishable by removal from the military. She was the first admitted homosexual I had met while in the Army. As I walked to my car parked across the street from my vast motor pool parking lot, I wondered why a sergeant of her rank would do something so stupid. But since she forced my hand, I followed policy.

I didn't know what to do about her, so once in my office, I called a Chaplain I knew who was stationed at Fort Ord, California. He and I have been friends since our assignments in division at Camp Casey, Korea, when I was a first lieutenant.

The Chaplain was familiar with situations when homosexuals were outed. He said confidently that she was probably put up to it by some other person who wanted to know if I was gay. The Chaplain advised me to report the incident to my battalion commander. I thanked him for that great advice and went to Battalion Headquarters.

When told, my battalion commander was very relaxed about the incident; but he was always calm about everything. He advised me not to do anything, stating, "You don't want to end her career over that, do you Cleo? I know her; she worked on battalion staff as our Signal noncommissioned officer. She is a good soldier."

He was right. I didn't have anything against her. I didn't know her, and since I was given the option, I didn't want to destroy her career, but I also didn't want her in my company. She had admitted an offense that was punishable under military law, therefore it was better that I didn't look as if I was helping to keep her secret. My battalion commander agreed to have her reassigned.

As I left, he said, "Keep smiling Cleo." This was a comment I had heard a lot during my military career, so I smiled.

Within a week, the sergeant was processed out and gone from my unit.

In October, less than four weeks after I took command, one of my soldiers reported his child missing. The soldier took his eighteen-month-old daughter to the local mall to celebrate his birthday. The mall was small—only about thirty boutiques, jewelry stores, and a movie theater. In his statement to Central Intelligence, the soldier said he turned away for a few moments, and when he turned back around the baby was gone.

Concerned for my soldier I spoke with him in my office. He sat across from me. As we talked, his gestures and his nonchalant, aloof attitude were disturbing. Given more details, I found his story hard to believe. Later, I was told the child's mother told police she didn't believe the baby was kidnapped; she believed the soldier had the baby. The mother begged him to bring her baby back.

During my short period in command, this soldier had been in trouble and was disciplined. Within a few more days he was pending another disciplinary action.

His performance was poor, he was late for formations, he didn't care about his appearance, and the previous commander took more than enough repeat disciplinary actions to put him out of the Army, but I gave him another chance and had him sent to the battalion chaplain for counseling.

Within a week he was in trouble again. The soldier's non-commissioned officers and the first sergeant recommended him for removal from service, and I agreed. He was put out of the Army.

Next there was a call for me to be relieved. Somehow, I found out a field-grade officer, Major McAfee—who worked in the division Materiel Management Center—stated I should be fired because my Shop Office had a large number of used vehicle engines that should have been turned in to the supply warehouse. In battalion staff meeting I agreed that if McAfee was right, I would get the problem fixed. But it was strange a major who didn't know me would suggest that I lose my job so early in my command.

The unit was working hard, and I was working at pace with it. Hours after the shops were closed and everyone had gone home, I was in my office planning for the next day and next month. My workdays were consistently fifteen or sixteen hours long.

During the same short sixty-day period, my battalion commander summoned me for counseling. He was concerned I was being too hard on my company.

The battalion commander said, "Some of your officers and noncommissioned officers are complaining that you are pushing them too hard. You are going to burn them out, and you don't want to do that, do you Cleo?"

I responded honestly, "Sir, we are working hard because the company is not mission deployable. I have a maintenance company, but my equipment is unserviceable. I have tens of thousands of dollars in excess property that belongs to installation Fort Hood, and about the same amount of excess authorized property. The appearance of our offices and barracks are below standard compared with the companies I've served with in the past. Many soldiers were not qualified on their weapons and in general the company was not physically fit."

The commander said calmly, "Yes, Cleo but you don't want to do it all at the same time. I don't want you to destroy the company."

I thought, *destroy the company?* But I said, "I won't destroy the company, Sir. I just got the last of my officers and new first sergeant. I always put my soldiers first, and I will not ask anything of them that I can't do."

He said, "Anyway Cleo, you need to relax, smile, don't take everything so seriously. Have you seen the Humphrey Bogart movie, *The Caine Mutiny*?"

"No Sir."

The commander continued "Well, the ship's captain, Bogart was so tense, that his unit couldn't take it, and they mutinied. Now you don't want that to happen, do you, Cleo?"

"No Sir, I wouldn't want my guys to mutiny, and they won't." I smiled because he asked me to in the past. The commander, often said, "Smile Cleo," for no conceivable reason.

When he had finished talking, I thanked him for his guidance and returned to the company. The battalion commander gave me something to think about, so I met immediately with my five chief warrant officers to seek their opinions and advice. Maintenance warrant officers are assigned as the command's technical advisors. In addition to the technical and mechanical expertise they bring to their various maintenance shops, I asked their advice and input when gauging everything that impacts shops operations and before planning concepts that change company operations. After some discussion, the chief warrant officers agreed the company was on the right course and that work conditions and unit readiness were improving.

I went to the maintenance shops to check on progress, make mental notes, and interact with my soldiers in their workplace. I walked through the motor pool and maintenance shop areas at least twice a week to see and talk with my soldiers and to make myself accessible to them. I was always amazed to see a young soldier working fully inside the engine compartment of an M1 tank or bore scoping an artillery cannon or replacing a shattered Humvee windshield. I respect who they are and what they do. They inspire me.

That evening I talked with my first sergeant who, like me, was confused by the battalion commander's concerns and comments. With the first sergeant's input I decided to continue company operations uninterrupted toward my goal of unit readiness and high standards.

Later, when alone, I reflected on the battalion commander repeatedly telling me to smile. He was not the first senior officer to have done that. Most of the time I am either listening or thinking when I hear "Smile Cleola." I don't understand why smiling is so important. I smile when it is natural. Smiling perhaps signals that I am happy or in agreement with them? I have worked with male officers who cursed, yelled, even called people out of their name without a smile on their faces, but I need to smile.

I was taught not to grin unnecessarily and not to exaggerate expressions of emotion. I am pleasant to everyone, but I am direct. I hold myself straight and dignified the way I was taught growing up. I wanted to fit into the battalion, have the commander like me, and appreciate the value I add to his command, but smiling or faking is not who I am. I am a serious person, but I love to have a good time, dance, sing, sew and cook. I am comfortable doing the right thing at the appropriate time.

I wanted the battalion commander and everyone to feel comfortable around me, but I would not smile all of the time just to improve my relationships. Standing at the mirror I created a facial position I call, "Cheekbones High." That is when I raise my cheeks as if I am about to smile, without showing my teeth. I tested it in staff meetings and Cheekbones High was a success. I didn't hear "smile Cleo" again, and I was happy about that. Cheekbones High was proven an effective tool without a significant sacrifice to my personality, and it made the commander comfortable.

CHAPTER 3

RAISE UP MAINTENANCE

———

"One, two, three, four," the Cadence Caller cried.
"One, two, three, four," the company responded.

The company was running in formation on our five-mile Friday run, the guidon flying in the warm morning wind as we paced along the back streets of Fort Hood. I ran out front, loving every minute of it. This was a dream fulfilled. The vision I had while in college at cadet Army Summer Camp, watching the large strong Airborne companies rock down Longstreet at Fort Bragg. I imagined myself leading a formation; now, I was doing that, and my soldiers sounded off loud and motivated. Fitness is integral to unit readiness and my unit was getting ready!

We were a unit to be proud of, and I was proud of it.

As the cadence caller kept us rocking, I saw my first sergeant out of the corner of my left eye. Soldier care was his highest priority, and he included me and the other officers on his list. He was great! We didn't want for anything. He and I worked together like a hand in glove. We kept each other informed; I literally told him everything because I never wanted anyone to catch him off guard, and he needed to know everything to do his job. He was a hands-on, high-standards, soldier-first, get-it-done first sergeant, rolled into a nice guy. I barely knew the battalion command sergeant major, because my first sergeant was way ahead of him on everything and in every way. My first sergeant had worked hard to bring the company to standard—cleaning, painting, repairing, schedule training, inspections, formations, reenlistments, and on and on. The barracks were clean, and he was building a strong cohesive group of noncommissioned officers. The first sergeant really got the work done.

In a short period of time the two of us had statistically one of the two best companies in both the battalion and the DISCOM, and we knew it.

"Count cadence; delayed cadence; count cadence, count!"

Out the corner of my right eye I see our supply sergeant, Sergeant Howard, setting our pace. She manages all the property in the unit. She was key to getting rid of literally a tank maintenance bay full of excess and broken old desks, chairs, and other office and barracks furniture. She has a dry wit that I enjoy. She quietly jokes about her ability to make things happen, as she made them happen. She constantly assured me, "There is nothing that I can't do in supply Ma'am, nothing!"

Sergeant Norris, our administrative expert, was beside her in formation. The Orderly Room was his office. He typed everything and did it well. His was the first face visitors saw when entering the company, and he represented us well.

Specialist Lara was calling cadence, no, it was Sergeant Diez the motor sergeant. Lara was his parts clerk, and the motor pool had an excellent team of mechanics. The motor pool team, advised by Chief Warrant Officer Alando, had improved the company's vehicle readiness.

The company was doing so well I asked the first sergeant to come up with a company motto. The first sergeant and noncommissioned officers got everyone involved in suggesting a motto. Remembering the wrench mounted in the mountains over the Maintenance Battalion Headquarters at Camp Casey, South Korea, I made a suggestion. After a vote was taken, surprise! My suggestion won.

"Clap your hands, clap your hands, clap your hands, clap your hands."

"Clap, clap, clap," the soldiers clapped their hands as we ran.

The street was filled with units running. I saw the Echo Company's guidon. Echo Company was completing its run going back toward the battalion area. I held up my hand in recognition of the commander, Malia Lawrence. Mae's company was immaculate—without a doubt the best throughout the DISCOM in appearance and in performance statistics. Our company's Orderly Rooms were next door to each other, and I had a way to go to deserve to be her neighbor. My short-range goal was to get my company's performance levels equal to those of Echo Company. I told her I admired her leadership abilities; we were friends.

Mae and I met about ten months earlier when I introduced her to the assistant division commander support—part of my job when I worked as the maintenance officer on division staff. But we didn't associate a lot at work; we were too busy, and I was told it was unwise for Black officers to congregate at work for fear of causing tension or giving the wrong impression to other officers. Though I think it is ridiculous, I have actually heard some Black officers say, "I had better go, there are too many of us standing together," or something like that before walking away. That was funny to me and Mae. Personally, I share the opinion of Second Brigade commander, Colonel Gibbs.

Someone commented his predominantly Black staff was too black. Colonel Gibbs replied, "I don't care what is said about how my staff looks, the question is can they do the job?"

The answer was "yes"; he had an efficient operational professional staff.

Then he asked, "Has anyone asked the other brigade commanders about their staff?"

The answer was "no," and some have all White lead staff officers. That was hilarious! I was both surprised and pleased by his comments. The question is can they do the job? Yes, my belief is akin to his.

"One, two, three, four; two, three, four; two, three, four; two, three, four."

Anyway, Mae and I prefer our friendship to remain free of professional involvement. We prepared ourselves for attempts to pit us against each other and remained unphased by little jokes, jabs, and innuendos directed at either her or me to make one of us attack the other.

The truth: Mae was awesome at her job, and I was very good at mine, so why should we have been adversaries? My only comments about her were complimentary, and when comments were made about me to her, she smiled and acknowledged the speaker by saying, "Mmm, Hmm, I see," and let them talk.

A big difference lied in our command relationships. Everyone including Mae seemed close to our battalion commander. He was kind, pleasant, and I liked him, too, but I didn't know him very well, and I was not sure what he thought of me. His staff liked Mae; I was polite to the staff, but our relationship was strictly business. Since I'd held a Battalion Operations position, I frequently anticipated what would be needed next and provided them data before it was requested.

"Count, Cadence, count!"
"One, two, three, four!"

The mission side of the company was in good hands. All three of my lieutenants are super stars, but I didn't let them know it. I put everything I know into them. I wanted them all to succeed, and I ensure they were treated to feel equal when approaching me because I know how it feels to be left out.

If my Shop Office could have detached itself to become a commercial business, it would have been wealthy because of its efficiency. Lieutenant Hemsley, the shop officer, and his noncommissioned officer in charge had made the shop proficient and organized.

Performance of customer maintenance started with our senior warrant officer, Chief Warrant Officer Clarkston, who was responsible for quality control and customer interface. We don't have any problems there.

My maintenance shops pumped work out like a Jiffy Lube, job in, job out. If we had the repair part, the job would be fixed in a few hours. My other four chief warrant officers—Porter, Alando, Tyson, and Person—along with the noncommissioned officers, kept the soldiers working and learning their technical trade.

"Quick time, march! Left, left, left right."
"One, two, three, four your left right."

The run was over. I had to get ready for a meeting with the battalion commander in his office this morning.

On the 120th day of command, I scheduled an office call with the battalion commander. In our meeting, holding cheekbones high, I briefed the comparative status of the company at present to its condition when I took command. Every command indicator—physical fitness, equipment readiness, weapons qualifications, including discipline and esprit de corps—was significantly improved. "Sir, I want your confidence as a leader and a soldier. My company has greatly improved and will excel to be the best it can be."

The commander admitted to seeing tremendous progress during my four months in command. He shared that two of my warrant officers routinely updated him of changes in the company. He admitted to seeing noticeable differences and the unit was in good shape.

We discussed other issues that needed attention. Professionally, I thought we were in a good place.

When finished I said, "Thank you for your time, Sir." Then stated the company motto, "Raise up maintenance! Sir!" I saluted and walked out.

CHAPTER 4

ONE STANDARD

———

One big inhale and an equal exhale. After five months in command, I could finally take a break. I was enjoying classical music, a sonata. It hadn't been easy, but the company was in an increased state of readiness.

I had learned communications and standards are key to building a cohesive unit.

My meeting with newly arrived enlisted members was scheduled for the afternoon. I found that sharing my command philosophy, expectations, and standards benefitted unit discipline, and got everyone started on the right foot. I copied the one-on-one meeting from my first DISCOM commander while in Korea, and I learned to visit the inspector general's office before making changes that impact the soldiers. I believed seeking guidance before taking actions was better than answering immediately after a soldier complained. Communication of standards and consistency in their application creates a stress-free work environment.

One morning I met with my chief warrant officers. Chief Alando, in his capacity as the unit motor pool technical advisor, had identified designated cargo trucks for modification to become mobile maintenance shop vans. He explained the

Army designed our unit to mobilize and operate in that way. The officers discussed it, but no one could deny Chief Alando was right. Although it took some shuffling around, most of my trucks became shop vans. The Army had already developed the standard; all we had to do was follow it. So, as soon as our noncommissioned officers were informed and the lieutenants got their tasks, the modification of vehicles began.

Chief Warrant Officer Alando was a confidant and advisor who had my confidence, so as the meeting ended, I asked him to stay back to talk.

"Chief, this is a personal concern. Nothing I can do about it, but I want your opinion. Tell me what you think."

"OK Ma'am, I will try."

"Captain Kinnear, my predecessor in this command, left Fort Hood a few days ago to take the position as my assignment officer in Army Personnel Command, Washington, DC. It wasn't until now that I had given assignment officers a thought. In the past they were very helpful, but I am not sure about this guy. You saw the company when you got here? He handed it over to me, that way."

Chief Alando agreeably said, "Yes, that says a lot. The work areas were inefficient, and excess was everywhere."

"Yep, now he will be positioned to look through my record and place me in my next assignment. He will be the ordnance captain's assignment officer."

"What do you think of that, Captain Davis?"

"Well chief, I can't say I like it. I wonder why the Army allows our peers to manage our records. I am just seeing the danger of it. The rumor is that a logistics general officer is setting Kinnear up for success and that the same general had him placed in the 'career enhancing' job at Personnel command. Chief, I had not heard the term 'career enhancing job' until now. I don't remember it from the Ordnance Officer Basic Course. I was told a general intervened to have Kinnear placed in company command ahead of me and others. In the Ordnance Officer Basic Course, we were told, 'Assignments don't matter; performance is what will make the difference; just do your best where ever you are assigned.' Now, I know that was not true; some assignments are 'career enhancing' others are not."

Chief Alando, "Setting him up for success? Do you know the general?"

"I know who he is chief, I mean I have seen him. He was in the Corps Support Command when I arrived in the division. I think Kinnear was on his staff. I didn't pay any attention to the general until my supervisor told me that the general directed Kinnear to get the next logistics command in division. I don't understand why he would compromise Army standards by selecting one officer over all others. To me it seemed the general prejudiced the process in favor of one officer; he is the general of us all, and he doesn't know the rest of us."

"Well for sure Captain Davis, the general didn't come to this company to see how Captain Kinnear was performing."

"I don't think that is important chief. I was told that some subordinate officers follow a general officer from assignment to assignment to assure the subordinate officer's career success. The term 'fast-tracking' is used to describe how officers, in the 'ole boy' system, are accelerated through the system. I'm from the south, and I've heard the phase 'ole boy,' but not in a way that can be used in the Army; this is new to me. I believe Kinnear, a captain with six years in service, is now on the fast-track to a higher rank; if so, it is shameful."

"Does that discourage you, Ma'am? The Army is a serious business; we all need to continue to take it seriously. What you described does not make sense."

"No, chief I have too much to do to be discouraged. I will continue to work until I am recognized, the way I should in a system designed to be performance competitive. Look at what we have accomplished in a few months, chief; I think I am competitive."

"Yes, you have accomplished a lot in this company."

"Thank you, chief; thanks for your time. I just needed to think things through. I will see you in the motor pool later this afternoon."

Alone for a few minutes, I reflected on concerns I discussed with Chief Alando. It appeared the general had given Kinnear advantages over everyone else creating two standards: one standard for those who were chosen by a general, and the other standard for those who were not. In my political science course this would be likened to the "haves and the have nots." If this was true, the general's actions were discriminatory, degraded excellence, and carried a long tail of interference with the promotion process, influence, income, and eventually retirement pay.

I looked at my calendar then prepared to take a routine visit to the company work area after lunch. First, I stopped by the Armament Section to observe and engage the troops. The Armament Section repairs artillery pieces and associated artillery support equipment. Chief Warrant Officer Tyson's absence was immediately noticeable. His noncommissioned officer in charge, Sergeant Garcia was busy working in the maintenance bay with his guys. After greeting him and the troops, I asked inquisitively, "Where is Chief Tyson?"

Sergeant Garcia responded, "Ma'am, Warrant Officer Tyson leaves at 1500 hours to attend class."

I was moving my head up and down in recognition of what Sergeant Garcia said, but I was thinking, *What! Chief Tyson was the most selfish person in this unit, and he is abusing his authority.* The workday ends at 1700 hours. Warrant Officer Tyson complained he had to attend PT at 0600; now I find that he leaves work two hours early three days a week. He was lazy and placed himself before the mission and his troops. I didn't like it. Taking six hours off work per week for school while everyone else was working was unacceptable, but since the previous commander approved his class hours for this semester, I let Chief Tyson finish this semester.

This was the kind of behavior that would erode the cohesive environment I desired. Moving forward, everyone in this company would be held to one standard; no one would receive unjustifiable special privileges. Upon my return to the Orderly Room, I discussed Chief Warrant Officer Tyson with the first sergeant who agreed with me completely, and since all education requests were subject to my approval, no one would place civilian education before our military commitments. In January, Chief Tyson submitted a request for spring semester college classes that would require him to leave work for about seven hours per week. At first glance I knew I was not going to sign it. As I left the Orderly Room, I told Sergeant Norris I would be at Chief Tyson's office. Once there, I showed him the document and said bluntly, "Chief, I can't let you leave your job two hours before the workday ends, three days a week. That is six hours, and you want thirty minutes off two days a week? You are asking for seven hours off work per week? Think about your troops.

"Chief Tyson said, "My noncommissioned officer has things under control. There won't be any problems."

I shook my head from side to side, "Chief Tyson that isn't the point…You are taking off almost one-fifth of the work week. How do you justify your position if the Armament Section only needs you part-time?"

He said, "They can call me if they have a problem."

"No chief, I will not give you that much time off during the week. What you are asking doesn't make sense and you know the regulation; attending school is on your own time."

"But Ma'am the soldiers take classes during the day …"

Interrupting him, "Chief you are a leader in this company. Are you equating your college studies with enlisted soldiers attending the Basic Skills Education Program to improve English and math skills? Are you kidding? You know Basic Skills Education is only authorized during duty hours to assure soldiers attend. It is like a special duty."

His statement left me a little teed off. He was selfish, and it appears he was used to manipulating the system. While every person in this unit was working a minimum of eleven hours or longer a day (0600–1700 hours), he wanted time off.

Mr. Tyson whined, "Well, I am trying to get my degree. I need my education."

"I understand chief, and I will help you go to school as long as you can also do your job, but I will not let you leave your soldiers to do your work while you advance yourself at their expense. I don't have to give you any time off, but I will work with you if you reduce your hours away from your shop within reason."

Not giving him another opportunity to talk about his need for education, I changed our topic of conversation to the needs of his section and his soldiers. When I left his office I visited other maintenance sections, engaged soldiers in conversation and admired their skills before going back to the Orderly Room.

While driving back to my office, I decided to talk with the battalion commander about Mr. Tyson. The commander's secretary was out, and his door was closed, so I had a seat in the waiting area just outside his door. Unexpectedly, I overheard bits of a conversation between Chief Tyson and the battalion commander.

Chief Tyson said, "She said she is not going to sign to let me go to school, and I need these classes."

"Well did you tell her that you have been going to class in the afternoons to get your degree, chief?"

"Yes sir, I told her, but she doesn't want to hear what I have to say, Sir."

"Well, I will talk with her chief. I will tell her how it benefits the company to have another person with a degree."

"Yes Sir …"

The commander optimistically emphasized, "Education levels are a good indicator; she will have to see that."

Chief Tyson, "She just doesn't … I tried to tell her."

"Don't worry about anything Chief Tyson. Go back to work; I will take care of it, and I will call you later to let you know what happened."

"OK, Sir. Thank you. I really need these courses."

The commander, "I will call you after I talk with her."

"Yes Sir; okay, Sir."

I stood up as Chief Tyson stepped out of the door.

"Oh … Hey Ma'am."

I responded, "How are you, chief?" As he walked away, I knocked on the commander's opened door.

The commander looked up, "Come in Cleo. Have a seat."

"Thank you, Sir." I paused, "Full disclosure Sir, I heard some of your conversation with Chief Tyson, and I cannot let him go to school for seven duty hours per week."

"Well, Cleo it would benefit your company to have another person with a college degree."

"Yes Sir, you are right, but I can't let him take time off work to attend college, when I have numerous soldiers attending college and complying with Army regulations. Sir, who doesn't want to take classes during duty hours? I can't let everyone off to go. The regulation is the same for everybody and I will administer it equally except in unusual circumstances. If his classes were at 1700 hours, I would grant him time to travel to the class on time. But I can't let him consistently take hours off to sit in class while my privates are working. Chief Tyson wants special treatment, and I don't believe in that. I have to think of unit morale and unity. Sir, Chief Tyson is thinking of himself. I need you to help him understand his responsibilities to his soldiers, and the unit."

The commander still supporting the chief, "Cleo, you don't think he should get his degree?"

"Absolutely Sir, I hope he finishes college but on his personal time, like everyone else—mission permitting. I will approve classes he wants to take; I told him that before he came here to see you. It appears Chief Tyson came here to undermine my decision, and I can't let him do that, either."

The commander, "Well, if you have made up your mind, I guess that is that."

"Thank you, Sir. I think this is right for the unit and for Mr. Tyson, and I appreciate your support."

I stood, saluted and moved out smartly. I remembered to keep my cheekbones raised, and I recalled the conversation about the "ole boy" system. This is how it works, and I am sick of it! Some people have to work and follow policy, while others like my chief are gaming the system using a guardian or friend to move to the top. For him that ends today.

The following day I approved Mr. Tyson's adjusted education request form. Hopefully he learned this company has one standard for everyone. Our standards are consistent with Army regulations and policies, so all soldiers—including officers—can trust both the system and the integrity of their commander.

CHAPTER 5

WE WERE CALLED

Knocking on my open office door, my administrative sergeant spoke enthusiastically, "Ma'am, the battalion commander wants you in the Battalion Conference Room, ASAP!"

Looking up from the notebook on my desk, "Now, Sergeant Norris what is going on?" I looked at my watch to see it was about 1500 hours.

As I stood up, the sergeant replied, "I don't know Ma'am but one of my friends told me the division is on alert for deployment … but I don't know."

"OK, Sergeant Norris, tell the first sergeant where I am."

I will never forget that day, August 2, 1990. I rushed—almost ran—to Battalion Headquarters to hear what was happening. When I arrived the battalion commander's staff officers, command sergeant major and some of the company commanders were standing near their seats at the conference table waiting for the commander to enter the room. I took my place, too. A few minutes later, the room was called to attention; the commander directed us to sit.

Reading from a page he gave us the facts …

"Today, 2 August 1990, our division is called to become part of the United States operation to deploy forces in reaction to the Iraqi invasion of Kuwait." The announcement was surprising. *Our division is deploying? We are deploying!*

The commander didn't have more information at that time, so after a bit of discussion we were released to our units.

In the days and weeks to come we ramped our operational tempo exponentially, working fourteen to eighteen hours six days a week and as needed on Sunday.

The battalion commander held Deployment Preparation Meetings on a regular basis. Total focus was on mobilization. The decision to deploy the division's equipment from Fort Hood was an unexpected requirement to many units who planned to receive war time equipment in theater—the area where war activities take place. But thanks to Chief Alando's suggestion months ago, our equipment was ready.

Every soldier in my unit was performing to high standard. As the two forward maintenance companies packed to deploy, my unit picked up their mission until we were supporting every unit in division while packing out ourselves. I respected my soldiers and noncommissioned officers for being a strong, intelligent, professional team.

One day in battalion staff meeting, the battalion commander mentioned Malia Lawrence, stating Mae wanted to come back to the battalion to deploy with us when we went. She would be back at Fort Hood within a few weeks. He immediately had my attention and that of the staff because everyone liked Mae. She was smart, very good at her job, professional, and pleasant. It had only been a few weeks since she was seated at this conference room table with us as commander of Echo Company. She was presently attending Combined Arms Service Staff School—a mandatory course taught at Fort Leavenworth, Kansas.

The battalion commander explained, "Mae is asking for a position in battalion so that she can be with us when we deploy."

I listened, recollecting that he and Mae were close. Their cordial command relationship was in stark contrast to the strictly professional relationship he had with me. Yep, Mae would be a great asset to the all-male battalion staff.

The commander continued, "But I am not going to let her come back." He waited a second, "Now, she did a great job as Echo Company commander, and we really like Mae, but it is time for some other people to have a chance."

He could have knocked me over with a feather. He doesn't want Mae back in his battalion?

He clarified, "After all we have to be careful who we let command and have positions during this time because they will become the Army's future generals."

I was sitting straight up in my chair but looking down at the table listening to his every word. I couldn't believe he let me hear him say that. I looked around the room, I was the only Black company commander and the only woman company commander in his battalion. I thought to myself, *could he mean he has to be careful of me in command because I will become a general? Maybe he is saying that he wasn't going to let Mae come back to the battalion because it will make her competitive for general rank in the future?*

Later in the week, Mae called me from Fort Leavenworth to catch up on our deployment. I enjoyed hearing her voice as she shared, "I asked the battalion commander for a position at battalion headquarters when I get back."

"Yeah, I know. Are you sitting down, Mae?" I paused for a moment then continued, "In staff meeting a few days ago the battalion commander announced that you want to come back to battalion."

"In staff meeting, why?"

I continued, "I don't know it's confusing to me, too … and Mae, he is not going to let you come back."

Mae responded, "You know Cleo, I asked him to place me in any position, so I could return to battalion. I didn't think it was a big deal. We worked well together, and I just left a few weeks ago."

"Yes, I know. He said he likes you and that you did a good job … but then he added, he has to be careful because the leaders deploying will become the Army's future general officers. That statement surprised me, Mae. He seems to have connected your return to battalion with your career advancement."

Mae responded, "Girl please … so he is being careful, leaving me here? Careful because I may become a general? That is ridiculous, Cleo."

Shaking my head, "Yes, ridiculous but that is what he said." Chuckling I continued, "Oh yeah, he also said it was time for him to give someone else a chance. It's as if he was talking in code."

"A chance to do what?" Mae questioned, also chuckling.

"Who knows? I answered, "The chance to work on battalion staff where they really need you. They all need help. Have you talked with him? What excuse did he give for not bringing you back?"

Mae responded, "Nope, I have not heard a word from him, but I haven't received orders yet either, so I'm not sure where I'm going."

"Maybe he is looking for a position for you in the Materiel Management Center or DISCOM Headquarters.

Mae answered, "I wanted to go with the battalion because my experience there can help the staff and support the companies, but I'm not going to worry about it. I will be just fine wherever I am."

"You're right about that; not having you will be our loss."

Mae ended our conversation to return to class, and I returned to work. A few weeks later when Mae returned to Fort Hood, she was assigned to division Headquarters Rear, the part of the headquarters that remained at Fort Hood.

LACK OF CONFIDENCE

A few company commanders were relieved for "lack of confidence." Rumors suggested their units were not performing to readiness standards sufficient to trust their leadership in combat. I guess Division wanted the best people in charge, but seeing a Black officer I know removed from command was hurtful and concerning.

I recalled my battalion commander said, "Cleo you are pushing the company too hard …" If I had listened to him my company would not be ready, and I possibly would be on the relief list. Meeting standards is never the wrong thing to do. Now ten months later the unit was trained and ready to go.

My three chief warrant officers—Porter, Tyson, and Clarkston—allegedly asked to have me relieved from command because of their concerns of deploying into combat with me as their commander. Hearing of their allegations, I set up a meeting with the three of them in Mr. Porter's office at the mechanical maintenance shop.

As I walked across the motor pool area, other members of the company were busy repairing customer equipment while packing and loading sets kits, outfits, and equipment for deployment. I waved, smiled, and greeted them, but my mind was on what was to follow. I was tired of these chiefs, their alleged secret meeting with my rater, and their fixation on undermining my authority; today would be our day of reckoning.

So much was happening, yet I had to take time to talk to these guys … while everyone else in the entire division, worked.

Entering the office, someone said, "Attention."

I walked in, "Carry on …" I took a seat, and we all sat and exchange greetings.

I continued, "You complained that you don't want to deploy with me as commander?"

Chief Warrant Officer Porter spoke up clearing his throat, "Yes, Ma'am, I said that because I don't feel safe going to combat with you as my commander. You are alright here, but I'm not sure you can handle it in when the pressure is on. I believe you will fall apart under pressure. I just don't trust you to command in combat." He paused then added, "I don't have to go anyway; I can retire."

As he talked, I thought, *Look at that coward. He has never seen me fall apart nor anything close to it. He was using me to scapegoat his fear. He was afraid. What audacity you have chief, questioning my strength. You don't know me … you don't know my people—the Edgar Davis family of Jefferson County, Georgia, descendants of slaves, we don't faint easily … and do you know my Father, who is the Most High? He will see me through. What, Chief Porter you believe I will fall apart? No sir, not me … you! I am watching you fall apart right now, shaking in your boots while sitting at Fort Hood. You are showing yourself, and what I see is a coward who is just a bit sexist!*

I responded calmly to Porter, "Okay, chief, got it."

Looking at Chief Tyson, "What do you have chief?"

"It's like what Mr. Porter said. You can't handle command in combat … and I don't want to deploy with you."

I answered, "Well, chiefs, this is how it is. I am not leaving this company. You can leave if you want, but I am not going anywhere."

Porter spoke up sarcastically, "I have twenty-three years in the Army; I am going to retire."

I shake my head yes, "Okay, chief."

Looking at Mr. Tyson, "And you Chief Tyson, are you retiring too? I'll sign your retirement request papers."

He didn't respond; he just looked at the floor. Tyson didn't have twenty years in service, therefore he would have to resign without benefits.

The third warrant, Chief Warrant Clarkston, seemed to be an observer. He stated he doesn't really have a problem with me as commander, stating "I have as much confidence in you as I would in anybody else."

That was a halfhearted compliment but good enough for me. We are about the business of fighting the nation's wars … so why are we playing games?

I responded, "Thank you, chief."

Then I said to Porter and Tyson, "I will be looking for your paperwork. Now let's get to work."

As I left the office with Chief Clarkston, I asked about the volume of equipment coming from our customers … At that point every unit in division was our customer, and every shop in my company was busy. As we talked, he apologized again. He has more time in service than Mr. Porter but he was ready to deploy with his unit in service to his country, and I respected him for that.

Every soldier must be medically fit to fly, which means shots, dental exams, and medical fitness exams. All soldiers with permanent medical profiles must be reevaluated to determine their medical fitness to serve in combat. Mr.

Tyson had a permanent profile but had remained on active duty because his profile doesn't limit his ability to work. He visited my office one day to share he wanted his profile for back pain reevaluated for upgrade to profile number three status—medically not deployable.

Listening to him rubbed me the wrong way, "Chief, profile reevaluations and changes in profile status are for doctors to determine, but if you are assessed 'not deployable' with this unit, you will leave me with no choice but to submit documents for your appearance before a medical review board for medical discharge. If you are not deployable with this unit then you are not deployable with all other units, so I will not leave you both in the United States and in the Army. Your soldiers are deploying to war therefore I will not leave you here in uniform."

Mr. Tyson shrugged, "Well, Okay Ma'am," and left my office.

When I received Mr. Porter's retirement papers, I signed them, and he was reassigned to a replacement company to process out of the Army. Mr. Tyson did not submit retirement papers and deployed with the unit.

Our maintenance mission doubled and then tripled as division repaired its equipment for rail transport and road march to various ports of embarkation. As the forward support battalions stopped work to pack out, my company picked up their brigade support missions while continuing to support our customers and deploy one-third of ourselves known as the "Advance Party."

The company's Advance Party's mission was to perform maintenance in support of all division equipment as it was disembarked in Saudi Arabia. The team of personnel—led by my shop officer, Lieutenant Hemsley—was among the first to depart the United States. They were going to offload and setup our maintenance contact trucks, maintenance sets, shop equipment, and repair parts to begin repair of division equipment as it rolled off ship.

The last of my equipment and my division's equipment arrived at our port of embarkation in early September, and I road marched in my Humvee to see it off. My unit's recovery assets and maintenance contact trucks followed the last division equipment to port, providing route maintenance and pulling unserviceable vehicles to upload for shipment.

I was scheduled to deploy in the Main Body, the largest group of deploying soldiers. As unit personnel deployed, work remained to be done: evacuating unserviceable equipment to installation maintenance activities and transferring installation property—buildings, linens, and even room keys from my hand receipt back to Installation Fort Hood. After scheduling a day to pack out my household for placement in storage, I took a break.

I usually talked with someone in my family every day, but today my mother's call was to tell me to come home because my dad was hospitalized. While in Raleigh, North Carolina— on leave for two weeks—the Main Party departed Fort Hood.

My mental situation's shift from combat deployment to my critically ill father caused me panic. I am close to my parents and my family. When I arrived home my dad was in a private hospital room; I visited and we laughed and talked. He was in good spirits when saying, "Cle you made captain, Captain Davis! Look at my little Black gal, I am proud of you Cle."

I responded," Thank you, Daddy. I remember what you told me about working hard and getting up early. They can't out work me."

Others in the room joined in the conversation, so our moment ended. Someone always stayed in the hospital with Dad. His sisters and brother visited from Georgia, and he was happy to see them.

A few days later, on Sunday after church, we returned to find my dad in intensive care. He aspirated after breakfast and was unconscious. In a family meeting with his doctors, they informed us he had a one percent chance of surviving his illness. They explained that his chance could improve with surgery, but he may be unable to process the anesthesia and remain asleep.

My mother had a family meeting in the hospital chapel. We prayed. Mama gave everyone a chance to speak. We decided to let him have surgery. I stayed in the chapel to pray alone.

Daddy survived his surgery. We were waiting for him to wake up, but he didn't. Members of my family took turns staying at the hospital day and night. I couldn't sleep, so I stayed at night. The intensive care waiting room was a somber place; I formed friendships, and we prayed for our loved ones together. We had the opportunity to visit every hour. Each time, I prayed and talked with Dad about good times.

One morning at sunrise, he opened his eyes. I said, "Daddy can you see me, it's Cle, I love you," and smiled. He went back to sleep.

I didn't know what to do. I was sad and hurt. Do I stay at home, give up hope, and wait for Dad to die, or do I go back to work and believe the doctors are wrong and wait for my dad to get well?

While alone at home I asked my mother for guidance and advice. She is a strong Christian woman, who in African American tradition ran her household, raised her children, and made final decisions. She was the backbone of this family.

Explaining my situation to her was sobering. She had no questions for me and said, "Cle, go back to work. Staying here will not change anything but going with your company may make all the difference."

So, with a heavy heart at the end of my leave, I flew back to Texas in time to pack out my household goods. Walking around my empty house, I was empty. I laid on the floor and prayed. I called the only man I have ever loved to speak with him once more. I awakened as sunlight filtered through the skylights in my living room and got dressed to leave my house for the last time until I returned from deployment.

On post, I turned in my civilian vehicle to Installation for storage. Two duffel bags contained everything I had. I called home every day to check on my dad and my family. I prayed he would pull through.

My office was empty; my first sergeant had my things packed for me while I was on leave. My noncommissioned officers shuffled me and everyone to the right place at the right time until finally we arrived at Gray Army Airfield, an Air Force station next to Fort Hood.

The plane doors closed, and we lifted off aboard the last commercial flight carrying my division's units. I reclined my seat, closing my eyes. I was of two hearts—clouded with the unknown and hope—so I prayed and began mentally composing a song I call "Genesis." The lyrics flowed as I heard the melody, "In the Beginning there is God before the Heavens, before the earth … In the beginning there is God … He is the Alpha and the Omega, the beginning and the end. Let's give Him Praise, Hallelujah."

CHAPTER 6

CLOUDS ARE ALWAYS FORMING

———

We arrived in Saudi Arabia under cover of darkness. The bus stopped next to a gigantic warehouse located at the port where our vehicles would arrive. A soldier picked up my bags and directed me to a cot. At least half of the battalion of about 400 people was bunked cot to cot, head to toe.

At dawn—after a short rest—I awakened to see a giant orange ball consuming the horizon framed by huge hanger doors. The sun, larger than I had ever seen, was emitting temperatures in the low eighties.

At battalion meeting later that morning, the battalion commander was disturbed by the absence of the battalion's executive officer who was expected on my flight. I shared I saw him at Fort Hood but he was not on the plane with me. The commander directed his staff to find the executive officer. The battalion commander was rumored to have given the executive officer an ultimatum, to be on the next available flight or suffer the consequences. "Failure to report" is punishable under the Uniform Code of Military Justice and can be career ending. I wondered why the commander was trying so hard to force him here, when many people who want to come were left at Fort Hood.

Lieutenant Hemsley and my unit Advance Party continued to conduct direct support maintenance for all division units as equipment was disembarked and claimed by a unit. Ships containing division unit's final pieces of equipment were scheduled to arrive within a week. The last of my company's equipment was meant to arrive then.

My troops who had lived in the staging area warehouse for weeks were anxious and ready to set up in the field. It seemed like forever, but after a few days the battalion receives an order to move from the staging area to a marshalling point in the desert about fifty miles away.

It was mid-October 1990; I had years of desert training under my belt and used every bit of knowledge from numerous National Training Center rotations. The vastness of this desert was humbling and beautiful; its greatness was distinctively different from the hilly desert at the National Training Center in California, but I felt at home—confident.

The Shop Office opened for business, receiving unserviceable equipment and providing recovery before the company was completely set up. At the same time, the Advance Party remained at the port repairing all division equipment as repair parts were received.

I attended the first sergeant's formations and visited work sections as time permitted.

Australian showers (water filtered through a shower head as it is poured into a canvas bag) were our only bathing source, and we happily indulged in that rare opportunity. Laundry was hand washed in an Army-issued plastic wash bowl and hung to dry on tent rope or whatever was available.

Field latrines and a mobile kitchen trailer were set up at the appropriate downwind distances from quarters.

The sun would drop suddenly, and blackness would cover us quickly ending the work day. Our power generators were shut down about an hour after sundown leaving the camp in celestial darkness. In blackout light, I retired to my quarters which was a small, general-purpose tent just up slope from my office tent. Tent life was teaching me the meaning of the expression, "It is lonely at the top." Once I secured my tent from light exposure, I was isolated. Little sand mice hopped around the edge of my tent entertaining me by dim flashlight. Rolling into my sleeping bag I zipped myself in before playing a cassette on my small tape recorder. In darkness, the music gave me comfort as I started praying for my family and my soldiers … for strength and wisdom, and for peace.

I BELIEVE IN YOU

Like a storm cloud cast a shadow over the earth's surface, unexplained catastrophic, nonsensical, or frivolous events occurred with sufficient consistency to exacerbate my day. One morning, the military police arrived at the company to investigate one of my youngest soldiers for possession of an illegal substance. The allegation against the soldier was vague, and I found it unbelievable. After talking with my first sergeant, I walked over to speak with the soldier in his living quarters. I put him at ease; we sat on cots across from each other. He appeared nervous and uncomfortable. I asked him to tell me what he thought was happening.

His face was strained, "Ma'am, I don't have any drugs, and I don't know why the military police are looking at me."

The contents of his duffel bags lay scattered over his area and on the ground, still there from the search conducted earlier in front of his squad leader and military policemen. Nothing was found in their search. Sitting amid his things, the private said, "I don't know why they think I have drugs, Ma'am. It is like someone wants to place a dark cloud over me to make me look bad. I don't understand it, Ma'am, because I haven't done anything."

I asked who sleeps in the cots near him, but I didn't suspect anyone. This was obviously a mistake because the private would not have means to get drugs in the desert. The unit had received mail from the United States, but this private had not received any mail.

I talked with him for a while to calm him and lift his confidence. Ending our conversation I stated, "If you have done nothing wrong, don't worry. I believe in you, and I promise to get to the bottom of this. We are at war, and I need you; your country needs you strong and alert. Trust me to find out what happened, *Hooah*!"

He snapped to salute, "*Hooah!* Raise up maintenance, Ma'am."

To assure the company was drug free my first sergeant conducted a 100 percent check of all personnel and property for all contraband. Results reported no contraband found. The incident was reported to battalion, and that was the end of it.

The desert was an amazing place. In the middle of the day, off in the distance, I could see sand clouds forming, blowing in our direction. Sand clouds sometimes were so dense I couldn't see an inch in front of my face even wearing goggles; to breathe I wore a bandana to cover my nose and mouth, and the wind was so loud that oral communication was impossible. Maintenance work was placed on pause until sandstorms passed leaving fine dust granules on everything.

The environment was desolate, but we were adjusting and working hard.

I'M HUNGRY

The battalion received the order to move to a different location. I tasked Lieutenant Hemsley with the responsibilities of planning and moving the company to our new site. It was good training for him and my other two lieutenants. The night move was smooth. At daybreak the unit sat perfectly within one and a half grid squares, organized—allowing vehicle traffic to flow in a circle without disrupting our company operation—and next to other battalion units. Relocating, packing and unpacking, and tear down and set-up burned additional calories.

Some of my soldiers lost between thirty and forty pounds in just a few weeks. Food was running low; even meals ready to eat were limited. We were issued MORE meals, something I didn't know the Army had in its inventory. A MORE meal is a small precooked containerized bowl of food.

A friend from the Ordnance Advance Course, Dia Berman—in her capacity as corps rations officer—stopped by to see me during a business visit to the division rations point in my battalion's Alpha Company. We had a great talk. Seeing a friend was good. Before leaving she gave me her grid coordinates and invited me to her place where she said there would be plenty food. I promised to come by.

Within a few days my driver and I traveled across the desert to her location about forty-five minutes away. After our greetings and a short talk outside, Dia took me to her office which was literally surrounded by food. I couldn't believe my eyes; *wow*, this was great! Their refrigerator vans were full of the commissary's finest fresh meats, fruits, and vegetables.

She offered me anything I wanted, stating, "This food is here for the soldiers; my job is to make sure they are fed."

I didn't need coaxing. What were the chances of this happening, that in this immense desert a maintenance officer—who was my friend—was in charge of food when my guys were hungry? We laughed and talked while my driver loaded the Humvee with all it could carry. What a blessing! I was thankful.

Cheerfully we drove back to the company carrying A rations (fresh fruit, eggs, bacon, chickens, cooking oil, flour, sugar, and seasonings) and boxes of B rations (dehydrated shrimp, potatoes, pork chops, beef patties, other dried foods, and canned vegetables).

Entering the company area, I was excited at the thought of feeding my soldiers. I had my driver go directly to the first sergeant with our vehicle's valuable treasure.

Later, I stopped by to talk with the cooks at our mobile kitchen trailer. The smell of fried chicken greeted me as I approached. "Fried Chicken tonight, Chef?" Chef was my nickname for my head cook.

"Yes, Ma'am," he was enthusiastic, "Fried chicken tonight!"

I asked if we have adequate cold storage to keep our fresh meat and eggs. He assured me that his coolers and ice box could keep fresh meat for about a week. My soldiers were happy; therefore, I was, too. That evening we had a feast! Chef and his team prepared cake, canned vegetables, salad, bread, and Kool-Aid to complement our fried chicken entrée. I ate the first meal in days. At days end everything was delicious, and everyone was full. Settling on a mound of sand, I watched as a small cloud illuminated black against the setting sun on our endless horizon; at home I would think a storm was forming. And maybe it was.

Soldiers talk, and some of my soldier's bragged about the evening's dinner and omelets for breakfast to others in the battalion. I received a message stating the battalion commander wanted to see me. He seldom called for me. Wondering what was going on I rushed to put on my load-bearing equipment and hurried through company security to Battalion Headquarters. Entering his van, I was announced, and I saluted. He told me to have a seat. I took out my notebook.

"Yes Sir," I sat down.

He said, "I heard your soldiers had chicken for dinner last night." His manner was subdued, "I want to know where the food came from."

I happily told him everything.

Then he said, "How do you think other division soldiers will feel when they find out your soldiers are having fried chicken for dinner?"

His tone seems aggravated. Holding my face, cheekbones high, I thought, *Is this man crazy? Who would turn away the chance to get hot food for their hungry soldiers?*

I said "Sir, we were starving. Some of the soldiers are losing weight at a fast rate, and MORE meals were not providing enough food. I had the opportunity to get some food and couldn't pass it up … and honestly Sir, I didn't think about other division soldiers—just my mechanics working in the heat melting away because they were hungry. Until Dia visited me, I thought there was no food in theater. She is from Fort Bragg and has lots of food for her Corps and all her units are eating. I didn't see a problem with getting some food for my guys."

Getting this food was not illegal, immoral, or unethical, so why was he upset about it?

He said something about the division's food cycle and limits placed on food that was ordered.

"Sir, my cooks pick up rations as scheduled, issue them then the soldiers eat them. The food we had last night was given to me by a friend. It shouldn't affect the ration cycle, and she accounted for it at Corps."

I understood him, the rations warehouse at Alpha Company and Materiel Managers at the Management Center were constrained to order within the division's ration cycle. But the division rations cycle doesn't limit me from getting additional food from Corps or any other American unit. I would have taken food from an Air Force, Marine, or Navy unit if they had food to share. I didn't understand why we were talking about food.

I listened to what he was saying, but it seemed he was nitpicking. Getting food for my troops was a good thing.

"Sir, I don't believe any other officer in my position would have turned down that food. We were hungry."

I think he knew what I said was true. No leader would have passed on that food under our circumstances. Why let my soldiers suffer when they didn't have to?

Then it dawned on me; Dia stopped by the ration's warehouse before her visit to me. Alpha Company should have a list of what was in her warehouse. Maybe the battalion commander knew about the food at Corps. Maybe, but I don't want to think about it. Anyway, I didn't regret getting food for my guys.

I promised the commander to stop my soldiers from boasting about our food to other soldiers, and because I still had days of rations remaining, I offered to share those rations with the other battalion units.

I was happy to invite everyone to eat.

"We will have fried chicken again tonight, and, Sir, one night we will have shrimp! We probably have enough for the entire battalion because I got boxes of food."

So, we reached a good compromise. I left satisfied that my soldiers would have a few more hot meals, and other soldiers could eat, too. At the company, the first sergeant and the chef worked out a feeding plan for anyone who wanted to eat. Later that day, through the opening of my tent I saw a long line of soldiers in tactical formation, moving to eat at the mobile kitchen trailer. The soldiers were happy; today was a great day.

IT CAME BACK TO HAUNT ME

Routinely, my first sergeant placed newspaper clippings on my desk. One article from a local Fort Hood newspaper yielded a disturbing update. The remains of an eighteen-month-old baby allegedly lost in the mall the year before were found buried near the III Corps and Fort Hood sign at the front gate. The first man I chaptered out of the Army was arrested for murder. The article further explained the ex-soldier turned himself in and confessed to killing the child. He told authorities where to find the body. I remembered his guilty facial expression, his arrogant and cavalier demeaner while telling me about his final moments with his child. Intuitively, I believed he killed her. The article was a source of sadness and gladness.

My mind wanders … that baby was buried in plain sight. Hundreds of cars passed her little grave every day. I passed her many times; I'm sure her killer passed her too. She didn't stand a chance against that heartless man, and her mother—I am so sorry for her. Maybe now both mother and daughter will have peace. Mournfully, I paused to pray for all involved, including the murderer, and I thanked God for giving me the wisdom to chapter him out of the Army.

YOU SHOULD HAVE TOLD US HOW

Within days of the food controversy, a helicopter landed inside my company perimeter. Just as I got to my Humvee en route to greet the visitor, I saw the battalion commander's vehicle coming through the abutting battalion perimeter. Simultaneously, Battalion Operations called my Orderly Room to inform us the assistant division commander support was landing to visit the battalion commander. I watched them exit my company area. Later, the Humvee returned to the helicopter, and it departed.

That evening, I received a message informing me the commander would visit my company the following morning; no reason was given, but he never visited, so it had to be something special. I informed my officers to be ready to brief their respective areas. My first sergeant took care of everything else. My officers were always ready to brief their sections. Setting the example, I kept updated company briefings ready—one on butcher paper, standing on a briefing easel, and another in a briefing notebook for deskside briefings.

The next morning after breakfast and formation, the battalion commander arrived in his vehicle. The battalion commander was generally pleasant, meaning nice, and always calm.

I greeted him and escorted him inside my office.

Seated, he asked, "Why did you set your company up this way?"

I didn't understand. "Why did I set up this way, Sir?"

"Yes."

He literally meant why I positioned the company the way it is.

I explained, "I used techniques learned as the forward support battalion, operations officer, and division maintenance officer during training for National Training Center rotations, and from field exercises in Korea."

I was upbeat as I explained why my sections were spread out and how we established security. I shared my desert field manuals. Not knowing what he wanted, I showed him some of the procedures I taught my lieutenants so they could learn how to set up in a desert environment.

He said, "The general told me to come over here to receive a briefing on how to set up in the desert."

I didn't say anything because I didn't know what to say. If I were a cartoon character my eyes would be bulging out of my head, and my head would be spinning. I knew something was wrong, but how did I get involved between him and the assistant division commander support? I didn't know the general; he was new, so he didn't know me, either. I became uncomfortable, and my nose and hands were sweating. Why was he putting me in this situation?

He stated, "Your company made the battalion look bad."

I just couldn't say anything; I had set up the same way since we left the port, and he could see my unit set up from his vans. My heart sunk because I felt somewhat bad that the commander was embarrassed by the general.

He continued, "So Cleo, if you knew the battalion was positioned too close together, why didn't you tell me?"

He was right. I knew the battalion's set up was hideous. Units were too close together and everything was on top of each other. I estimated all warehousing; vehicles; living quarters; mobile kitchens; latrines for Alpha, Bravo, and Charlie companies; and the battalion headquarters company were crowded within less than two grid squares. It was a clustered mess, like a slum. Echo Company was tight together, too, but it was much better spread out than the others. I tried to think of a tactful way to respond.

Again, he asked, "Why didn't you tell someone the area was set up wrong?" Oh, my goodness! It was the way he was saying it, as if I was responsible to tell him, his majors, and my peers how to set up. I wondered why he was doing this. He knows they wouldn't listen to me, and it would cause confusion.

I answered him honestly, "Sir the thought of telling anyone to reorganize never crossed my mind, but if I had, do you think anyone would have listened to me? I don't want to cause a problem or step out of place. I'm training my lieutenants to do what I know. I don't think your staff will be open to training from me. I don't want to step on anyone's toes, and I would have clearly been out of my lane. I was trying to be considerate."

He interrupted, "You have to be a team player, Cleo. We have to be a team to get things done." Again, speaking as if I had authority to correct members of his staff.

To bring things to an end, I said, "Sir, I hate this happened, but I don't believe the staff is open to my suggestions. If you want, I can help to reorganize the battalion now."

We talked a little longer, then he asked me to ride with him around my perimeter. I explained my set up to him. At the security point, I got out of his vehicle and saluted, as he rode away.

When I got back to the Orderly Room, my first sergeant couldn't believe what I told him. I felt bad about the whole thing until the first sergeant reminded me that the other company commanders should have known the proper way to set up as I did.

I realized my first sergeant was right. He chastised me for doing what was right, instead of counseling the two majors and other captains on staff who set up wrong. Anyway, I gave the battalion commander a quick tutorial and references.

I did my best to avoid conflict with everyone. I didn't want to fight, so I kept our interactions professional, free of clouds and confusion.

YOU HAD BETTER FIND IT

While on a mission, two soldiers took unauthorized liberty to visit the phone center. When they came out of the building, their Humvee with equipment was gone. Borrowing access to a mobile phone, the soldiers reported the vehicle missing to Shop Office. The shop officer and my first sergeant informed me after they called the military police and battalion operations. The Shop Office noncommissioned officer in charge sent a vehicle to pick up the soldiers.

I called a meeting with my lieutenants and select senior noncommissioned officers to develop a search plan. Looking at a map we established areas for reconnaissance. While I was talking, I looked at their faces, and everyone seemed willing to take on the challenge of finding one vehicle in the literally tens of thousands on that desert. My final comment was, "You will find it … bring that vehicle back". I spoke with authority and confidence.

Lieutenant Cooper said, "We will do our best, Ma'am. *Hooah*."

He and Lieutenant Johansen saluted and said the company motto. As my search team vehicles disappeared through our security point, peace overtook me; I knew they would find that vehicle.

Within the hour, the new DISCOM commander was announced coming through company security. He literally took command last week. I went out to meet him and saluted. Stepping out of his Humvee, he returned my salute while stating in a very stern tone, "What are you doing losing vehicles?"

I couldn't say anything.

He continued, "Well, you had better find it. You had better find it."

I responded, "Yes Sir, I know we will find it. The military police are involved, and company teams are searching for it right now. We will find it."

He said, "You better—you had better find it." My mind went back to the DISCOM commander in Korea who came into the position determined to get rid of Black officers. They looked alike, older men with gray hair, not fat but a bit disheveled. He made his disdain for me known. He was upset, and so was I because the vehicle was lost due to my soldiers' negligence and lack of discipline. As commander I was responsible, but the open threat from the commander was unnecessary and demeaning. I think he wanted to frighten me, but I was not afraid; I just looked at him.

As he seated himself back into his vehicle, he said, "I don't care what you have to do … you had better find that vehicle!"

I said, "Yes Sir, we will."

He drove off with me standing there.

Cannibalized vehicle frames were all over the desert. American military units were stealing vehicles to strip for spare parts. Thousands of miles of desert spread in all directions; vehicles moved about from numerous divisions, but I believed the vehicle would be found. I laid face down on my cot and prayed.

A few hours later, the shop officer called to talk on our landline in the Orderly Room tent.

I said "Yes, L.T. what's up?"

Lieutenant Hemsley said, "Ma'am, are you sitting down? They have found our vehicle."

I answered, "Oh my goodness! Where is it?"

Hemsley continued, "Some of our customers saw our Hummer sitting in the desert, unattended, and gave me a call. They stayed with it until members of our team took possession. The vehicle was operational, and they are on their way back."

I responded, "That is great news L.T. Thanks so much." Shaking my left fist, I thought, *Thanks. Praise God! Thank you, Lord.* Continuing I said, "L.T. don't tell anyone we have found it before it arrives. Thank you so much."

Hemsley said, "Exactly, no problem, Ma'am. *Hooah!*"

Immediately, I told the first sergeant. Forty-five minutes later, before dusk, I saw the vehicle coming through company security.

I said aloud, "*Hooah! Hooah!* Thank you, Jesus." Usually abandoned vehicles are vandalized for spare parts but our vehicle was recovered intact. I was so thankful that I gave myself space to allow for praise and celebration before I called the DISCOM commander.

"Sir, my Humvee has been recovered, and it is operational. It is being inspected for serviceability."

He said, "You found it?"

I repeated calmly, "Yes Sir. It is undergoing a technical inspection, but it is operational."

The DISCOM commander replied, "Well, I'll be … that is good. That is good. You say a customer found it—well, that is good."

I responded, "Yes, Sir. Just want you to know, Sir. *Hooah!*"

He was mean, but my victory is in my faith. I prayed from memory, adlibbing New King James Version: Mark 11:23–24 ***"For assured, I say to you, whoever says to this mountain, be removed … and does not doubt in his heart but believes that those things will be done, he will have whatever he says.***

CHAPTER 7

RED CROSS

On November 6, 1990, the battalion operations officer, Captain Jason, knocked on my door and entered my office area.

He stated, "The battalion commander sent me to tell you—a Red Cross message is coming letting you know your dad has taken a turn for the worst. You are needed at home because he is not expected to live."

My heart skipped a beat then sped up. I listened as he continued, "I mean, you already knew that, so what's new, right? But that is what he said."

"Thank you," I said without blinking an eye.

My mind was on overdrive as thoughts were running through it, but like an engine ceasing moving simultaneously in forward and reverse, I could barely move. I know my mother would not send me a Red Cross message unless he was dead. I needed to find a way to call home, to hear her voice … to hear her say everything was alright and that she was alright.

My first sergeant got my driver and vehicle, so I could find a phone. My first stop was Battalion Headquarters; but they didn't have the capability to transmit me home. So, we drove an hour to a Signal Unit that shoots directly to a satellite connecting to the United States. Anxious, on edge, and fearful, I felt sick.

Finally, I heard my mother on the phone, "Cle, we lost Daddy this morning …" I listened.

I said, "OK Mama, I am on my way. I will be there."

I was numb; I mean I didn't feel anything. I thanked the signal operator, and we drove back to the company.

My driver asked if everything was alright. I shared with him, "My father is dead." Hearing myself say it provided stabbing affirmation that this was happening.

He expressed sympathy. The ride back to the company was quiet; I was imagining what was happening at home. I needed to get out of there to be with my family.

My first sergeant contacted the battalion for my Red Cross message, but they didn't have it.

Hours seem to passed as I packed one of my two duffel bags and dressed in my least dusty uniform. I held a meeting with my officers and first sergeant to explain the circumstances. Lieutenant Hemsley was placed on orders as acting commander during my absence, so I filled him in on actions that must be completed within the next few weeks.

In late afternoon, I rendezvoused with the battalion commander at roadside to attain his signature on my leave request. I took fourteen days leave. I stood outside his Humvee door as he signed the form and expressed sorrow at hearing of my father's death. I thanked him.

Red Cross verification was needed before starting leave, and it still hadn't arrived. Since DISCOM Headquarters would receive the verification first, and DISCOM would be transporting me to catch my flight, I had my driver drop me off there to wait.

The DISCOM commander, who had been on the job for about two weeks, expressed condolences. It was dark and well into the evening before the Red Cross orally verified my father's death. I asked for the written Red Cross message because I really wanted it; somehow, to me, it would make everything official.

The DISCOM used a commercial vehicle to transport me to the US Air Force Base where I manifested on a C-5 tactical aircraft. I strapped myself in my seat and sat alone in the giant passenger compartment of the empty plane. The free movement of my seat rocked me to sleep.

I awakened many times during my flight; my sorrow increased as I neared my destination. Mentally, I recited the Lord's Prayer and Psalms 23 verbatim, while paraphrasing the New International version of Ecclesiastes 3:1–20, ***"Everything has a time, a purpose, and a season under heaven. Mankind and animals have the same fate; we both come from dust and to dust we all return."***

I recited these verses until I was literally in a space where I felt stuck in a void equally as far from home as from my unit in the field.

Memories of so many good times flew through my mind. So many Christmases, Father's days, and birthdays when we would wake him up to receive the same gifts—ties, cologne, belts, and socks—every year. He made good use of them because he always dressed in a suit or pants and sport coat. He always looked good and smelled good; his hair was always in place. He was justifiably a proud man.

During Sunday dinners we would listen to dad talk about his family when he was growing up, especially his grandpa, Bill. He always had funny stories about his grandfather's White relatives who accepted Bill but called my dad a nigger. Bill Davis and his Black relatives didn't care anything for their White relatives. Black people who were the products of rape then sold into slavery by their fathers had no reason to have affection for them. Daddy's grandfather and his father Edgar Davis and the whole family farmed land owned by a cousin. I am comforted by memories of my dad making us laugh as he told his stories.

I dozed to pass the hours. Finally, at Dover, Delaware I was processed through customs, given a commercial airline ticket, and released to fly home. People stared as I made my way through the commercial side of the airport. Still dressed in dirty desert battle dress uniform and tan boots, I called home to give my family my arrival time. Sad is not sufficiently strong to describe how I felt as my sister and brother picked me up at the airport. We didn't talk much on the way home. As the front door opened, I saw Mama, and we hugged. "I am so sorry Mama." I wept. It was Thursday already; I somehow missed a day.

I had to buy clothes because I don't have anything to wear, and I had lost two dress sizes.

The family viewing and wake were Friday, and the funeral and repass were Saturday. It was hard, every bit of it. On the next day, Sunday, I accompanied my brother-in-law to his father's retirement from the ministry. My sister wasn't able to go so I went with him because I wanted to celebrate his dad. The church service, farewell program, and meal helped me ease my pain.

Monday, my sixth day of leave, I started closing my dad's bank accounts even without a death certificate. The next days were spent ordering a grave marker. Everything was done and paid for except for that, so I ordered it. I know this was literally the last thing I would be able to do for my dad. Family members were leaving to return home; then suddenly my leave was over.

Travel time from my unit to North Carolina took two days, but because I was booked on commercial flights back into theater, my travel time was cut in half. I signed off leave at battalion operations on the Tuesday before Thanksgiving. I asked for my official Red Cross message, but it wasn't there. They claimed to have never received it.

My first sergeant had a driver pick me up. It was dark when I arrive at the company, so I went to my tent without talking to anyone but the first sergeant. The night was very lonely.

After formation the following morning, many of my soldiers approached me with hugs and sympathy. I was grateful, humbled, and thankful for every comment. When I entered my office, my lieutenant was waiting. He stood up, saluted, and said, "Welcome back, Ma'am, good to see you. I have a new appreciation for what you do on this job, and I am glad to go back to my office."

I asked what happened. He said, "Well, Ma'am. I am glad to see you back, wish you the best of health, and no more emergencies. Everything is caught up, so if you don't have anything for me, I will go back to my office and stay there."

I let him go. Later, my first sergeant confided the lieutenant was mistreated during a battalion meeting, specifically stating that one of the field-grade officers, Major McAfee called him an "Asshole!" because he stood up against attacks on the company. The first sergeant didn't have the whole story but between Hemsley's actions and what the first sergeant knew, I concluded the lieutenant was not ready for the vitriol at battalion meetings.

The first sergeant also shared that Chief Tyson told his troops he wished I had died instead of my father because he hated me and hoped I wouldn't come back. The first sergeant and I laughed. "He is miserable because he is lazy. He wants the easy way out of everything, a special standard just for him. I don't blame him for hating me."

At the battalion staff meeting I asked for my Red Cross message, but no one had seen it. None of my fellow commanders acknowledged my father's death; I wasn't even welcomed back. We certainly didn't understand each other. I had not done anything to any of them, they were following the lead of the battalion commander. I did my job, and it was done well; I didn't have time to get into their heads. My daddy taught me to work hard, be thorough, get up early, and finish what you start to be the best, adding that once you are the best, know that you are the best. He was right; I worked hard, I was the best, and they didn't like me for it.

I was moving on fumes, emotionally and physically. My soldiers were very supportive, and their energy motivated me to keep going. On Thanksgiving Day, two days after returning from emergency leave, I served my soldiers dinner, greeting each one as I placed turkey on each plate. I was upbeat and smiling, joking with the guys. I said with enthusiasm, "You can have all you want, *Hooah*, all you want. I serve seconds."

Talking to them helped me get through the day. I wanted my soldiers to have a family environment at Thanksgiving, and it seems everyone enjoyed the meal except me. I did not eat anything, taking this time to fast and pray.

Night was a cycle of napping sadness and prayer. I was so sad; my heart was so heavy.

SHE IS A GOOD TROOP

One day a friend filled me in on something he said was very important that I had to know… and, wow, what a bombshell.

Tick, tick, tick, tick … my mobile phone was ringing.

"How are you, Cleola? I am sorry to hear about your father's death. How was leave? How is your mother and the rest of your family?"

"Oh, hi Sir, how are you doing? I am Okay Sir."

"It is good to have you back."

"Good to be back Sir."

"Look, Davis there is no easy way to tell you this, and I only have a few minutes. While you were gone to your father's funeral, your battalion commander and the DISCOM commander visited division Headquarters to ask the one-star general, the assistant division commander support, for permission to remove you from command."

"Oh, my goodness, Sir. They did? Why Sir, do you know?"

"Supposedly, because the lieutenant who was acting as commander was inadequate. I don't know your lieutenant; is he adequate?"

"Sir he is a very good officer."

"Also, your battalion commander said he was uncertain that you would come back. And that he needed a dependable person in your position."

"Yes, Sir, I see."

"I don't know your lieutenant, but I know you. So, when they left, I asked the general to make them wait, to give you a chance to come back. Davis, we don't have a warning order, meaning we are not scheduled to move. I gave him my assurance that you would be back in a week, and here you are back within the week."

"Yes Sir, I am back; of course, I would come back."

"The general doesn't know you, but I told him that I know you—and think very highly of your work. You were highly regarded by my brigade commander, Colonel Gibbs, when you worked on this division staff. And the previous division commander told the brigade commanders that you had given him the best tactical briefing he had ever received from a logistician. And after your defense planning enabled the brigade support area to destroy an opposing force tank at the National Training Center; now that was rare, Davis … exceptional! After that training center rotation, the division commander told the previous DISCOM commander to put you in a command position. And the general selected you to represent the division when Public Broadcast Station, *Mac-Neil/Lehrer NewsHour* did a segment on women in combat last spring, and I recall that you represented us in Newsweek last summer. I wanted the general to know how outstanding you are."

"Thank you, Sir, for remembering how hard I've worked to be here and standing up for me. I will never forget this, Sir."

"I told the general, 'Sir, don't let them do that to Davis. She is a good troop, a good officer. She is just on emergency leave for another week. Give her the chance to come back next week. She will be back.' Those guys, especially your battalion commander, were wrong to do this … to remove a soldier while on emergency leave. The general agreed to give you the opportunity to return from leave, and you didn't let me down Davis; you are back."

"Thank you so much Sir. Thank you for believing in me. I don't know what I would have done if I had returned here to this desert, and they had stripped me from command."

"You deserved time to go home to bury your father, Davis. You don't owe me thanks. Excuse me for a minute. Oh, I have to go. Davis, you are going to be alright. Keep your head up. Be safe and take care of your company."

"Thank you, Sir. Thank you so much. Take care of yourself, too. Thank you."

'Good-bye."

"Thank you, Sir, good-bye."

Click, he hung up.

I needed time alone, so I drove to a place where there seemed to be no horizon. I just needed to breathe.

The conversation brought clarity to my somber reception by fellow company commanders and staff at staff meeting and Chief Tyson's comments—hoping I would die and not come back—but I am stunned to hear how Lieutenant Hemsley was cursed and sworn at. Hemsley was an outstanding officer. I believed his mistreatment was because he was assigned as my lieutenant, and that hurt. I didn't bring my officers into my situation with battalion because it had nothing to do with them. My lieutenants deserved a normal experience as company grade officers in the military, and I did everything I could to ensure they got one.

I wonder if they threw away my Red Cross notice hoping they would not see me again. Maybe they planned to remove me and have orders cut to keep me in the United States.

My commanders were obsessed with getting me out of command, and I knew why. The idea that I would become a general frightened them, but it was inconceivable to me. They couldn't accept the thought of me as a general officer and were punishing me for it. They were thinking about what may happen fifteen years from now while I was thinking about surviving tomorrow.

I sat quietly, opening the Bible; my prayer was from the King James version,

Matthew 6:9–13 ***"Give me this day my daily bread, and forgive my trespasses, as I forgive those who trespass against me."***

I forgave them.

CHAPTER 8

LIKE WILD DOGS

"Hi, Marilynn, how are you?" I answered my mobile phone.

"Hi, Cleo I need to talk with you privately, I have something important to tell you that can't be discussed on the phone. Meet me at this grid coordinate."

I wrote down the numbers …

"OK, see you in the time it takes to drive there."

After driving about ten miles to meet, my friend Marilynn and I hugged and greeted each other before leaning on the hood of her vehicle to talk.

"Cleo, I think they are planning to relieve you from command. Your battalion support operations officer—"

I interjected, "Major McAfee?"

"Yes, McAfee had nothing good to say about you and Lieutenant Hemsley at the materiel managers meeting with the DISCOM commander the other night. His comments were brutal! He was especially critical of your Shop Office operation. What is going on?"

"My Shop Office? Marilynn, he can't say anything negative about it. You see the reports; they are excellent and so is Lieutenant Hemsley. McAfee doesn't know what he is talking about. There is absolutely nothing statistically nor functionally wrong with my company's mission performance which is Hemsley's job. My guys are great, and my maintenance production reports are great. McAfee is crazy!"

"Girl, I'm just telling you … McAfee has a gripe with you."

"Yes, I know he does but I don't know why; I barely know the man." Then taking a brief moment to reflect, I continued. "And did you hear that Major McAfee cursed Lieutenant Hemsley in a meeting while I was on leave? One of my guys told me. Hemsley didn't say a thing, and that is good because I wouldn't have let McAfee get away with disrespecting my lieutenant. Hemsley speaks for me, and do you think McAfee would curse me in a meeting? Heck, no!"

Marilynn laughed, "But Cleo, you are missing the point. I don't think Hemsley and your maintenance shops are the issue, they want to relieve you."

"Yes, I know they want me out, but I guess they can't justify removing me. You don't know, they are constantly coming after me. My battalion commander and the DISCOM commander asked the general—the assistant division command support—for permission to remove me from command while I was on emergency leave. If not for the division operations officer's intervention on my behalf, I would have been removed from command for going to my dad's funeral."

Marilynn agreed, "Girl, isn't that the lowest? They are so dirty! I heard something about their visit to the general, too. Thank God for the operations officer. But that is not what I'm talking about. Something else is happening. This week they told my office mate, Captain Eric Greyson, to be ready to take command of your company. The DISCOM commander has met with him, and he is getting ready to assume command."

Placing my hand on my cheek, "This is so interesting girl-friend, because no one has said anything to me about leaving command early. I'm just completing fourteen months, and as you know, the standard time for company command is eighteen months. I don't know what comes next, but I believe my battalion commander has wanted to fire me from the start. Before we left Fort Hood, he commented that people in command and key positions during the war will be the next generals."

"Yeah, Cleo this is crazy. What have you done to them? You are good at your job, and you are strong. It doesn't make sense."

"Yep, but they hate me, and they don't want me to succeed. I learned long ago that some people don't need a reason to hate because they think hating is a right—their right to be exercised at will."

We stood quiet for a moment before Marilynn broke our silence, "Do you know Eric Greyson? He says he knows you."

"Yes, I know him. He was a nice guy. We worked together at a past assignment, and I like him, but not enough to give him my job."

Marilynn said, "You got that right!"

"I am a little perturbed by the ease planned for Greyson. He doesn't have to do anything to get what I've worked so hard for—like back to back rotations to the National Training Center, living in dirt for months. I counted the days, and within one year I was in the field and away from home a total of over five months."

Marilynn grunted, "Girl, that is too much."

Jokingly, I stated, "And you know, that is no way to have a social life."

Marilynn agreed laughing, "None! You have given up a lot."

"It is the 'ole boys' working the system. Without trying, Greyson becomes a man of privilege, handpicked to standby while a plan is contrived to force me out. This is disgusting. And unfortunately, they are passing their ways to a nice guy like Greyson."

"As I said, Cleo, they are the worst. All of them combined can fit their integrity into a thimble. You don't deserve what they are doing. No one does."

"I guess they are mentoring him. You know Marilynn, mentoring is the new buzzword for 'good ole boy,' making special exceptions and giving privileges to a select group intended to manufacture the success of those in the group. Leaders 'mentor' the people they want to succeed but don't necessarily mentor the people they lead. There is something oxymoronic about separating 'mentor' from the definition of 'leader.' That certainly was not taught in officer basic course."

Marilynn stated, "Girl, leadership—what is that?"

We laughed.

"Let's face it, they are racist. They believe a White man should have my command because he is White and therefore entitled. They justify discriminating and treating me unjustly because they are White."

"And you are a woman." Marilynn added.

Shaking my head, "Yes, and that too. It is a dirty game, and they are playing for keeps. So anyway, what do you think they are cooking up to throw me out?

Marilynn moved putting one knee on her vehicle bumper, "I don't know girl, your character and professionalism will not give them cause for your relief. So, get ready for something that will provide them a reason. Prepare for the unexpected."

"Prepare for the unexpected … those are words to live by. And this is under friendly conditions. These guys are supposedly on my side—the friendly forces, my chain of command. For no reason, they are hostile. They are vicious!"

"Yes, Cleo I know what you are saying. This is unbelievable to me, too, and I am not living it. I know this is hard, but you can make it. Just 'hang in there,' girl. Be strong and get ready."

"Thanks to you I will be ready, my sister. I know what I'm fighting, but who would believe racism from our country would be on the battlefield in a foreign country? No one prepared me for this."

"We fight the way we train; whether at Fort Hood or Saudi, people are the same." Marilynn stated words of wisdom.

What she said was profound. I should not have expected them to change.

"Well, I am not going to let these jokers bother me. I can't move until they move, and I won't know where to move until they do something, right?"

We chuckled. As we donned our helmets and goggles, I thanked Marilynn. We bid each other good-bye and departed in different directions just as the sun was lowering, casting long shadows to our rear.

Driving home, I reflected on my talk with Marilynn. These men were afraid of me; I was not afraid of them. They made me their enemy because … I'm a Black woman commanding in this division during combat. My presence infringed upon what they thought rightfully belonged to them. I believe their hatred was rooted in the belief that they were meant to vicariously inherit positions of leadership in the military and in the country at large.

They were afraid and paranoid that my success would alter their advantage. The audacity of these guys feeling entitled to my position because of their skin color!

Like a pack of wild dogs hunting prey, my battalion commander (the instigator) and the DISCOM commander (his facilitator) were conspiring to attack and destroy me. But I was not going down without a fight. I was not a helpless lamb in a bush. When the time comes, I will fight!

Turning into my company security point, I waved and smiled at the soldiers on duty. Seeing them made me happy. It was getting dark, and the first sergeant was holding formation. My driver took possession of my vehicle, so I could wait in the Orderly Room to see if the first sergeant needed me for anything. After we talked, the day was over. I walked up the slope to my quarters, laid on my cot, hummed a few hymns, and read a little scripture before going to sleep.

I AM FEARLESS

While working at my desk, I was disturbed by the sound of rustling at the canvas door to my office. When I looked up, Major McAfee—a big, tall man, about five feet four, 300 pounds—was towering over my desk.

I offered him a seat, but he refused, flipped open his notebook, and started reading.

"The DISCOM commander wants you to give him an hour long briefing on the status of your company."

The DISCOM commander took command less than two months ago in late October; I briefed him then.

Positioning myself to see his face I address him, "OK, I have a company briefing on butcher paper and a desk top briefing that I gave him during his orientation visit a month ago. Will either of them do?"

McAfee replied, "No, he doesn't want that. He wants you to brief using slides and projector in his briefing tent at DISCOM, Headquarters."

"Okay," I know this was what Marilynn warned me about.

He continued, "It will be at 2000 hours on 8 December."

Unphased by what he was saying, I put my pen down, leaned back in my chair, and crossed my arms, "OK, I see. And what is this briefing for? I mean what is the topic?"

The major stated eagerly, "Well, the commander has concerns about your quality control. Battalion has received complaints from your customers."

I heard him, but I was thinking that December 8, at 2000 hours is tomorrow night, only about thirty-two hours from now. My other thought was that if battalion received complaints why was I briefing the brigade-level commander at DISCOM and not my battalion commander?

Pushing him for more information, "And why does the DISCOM commander have concerns, Major McAfee?"

Fidgeting with his notebook his voice got stronger as if he was annoyed by my question, "I don't know … he said Quality Control."

Sternly but quietly I said, "Yes, you do Major McAfee … you do know." My response caught him off guard. "You have staff oversight of my maintenance shops, and you are causing the DISCOM commander's concerns, if there are any. I want you to know that I know it is you who is creating problems, hoping to hurt me."

I stood up, walked around my desk, passing behind him to get to my door, "But it is not going to work. You hear me? It is not going to work." I gestured for him to leave by pointing my finger to the doorway. "Is there anything else?"

As he pulled back the canvas to walk outside, I didn't say, "Sir," I didn't salute, and my cheekbones were not high.

When he walked a few feet, I repeated so he could hear, "It is not going to work."

I watched as he got into his vehicle and rode off.

I felt like these guys were uncompassionate beasts! Where was my rater, the battalion commander? The DISCOM commander was his boss. My chain of command was the battalion commander then the DISCOM commander. McAfee had no authority over me. He worked on the battalion staff. They were obviously coconspirators.

Thirty days after my dad's death, they were pulling these shenanigans. Maybe they don't understand what it was like to lose a parent, but emotionally I was at the lowest point of my life. This was unnecessary "bull" coming from their fixation on giving my command to a White man; not the best man because I was the best "man" … but a White man because he was White.

They didn't care what happened to me as long as I was not commanding. Everyone knew "relief for cause" was career ending. They planned to create a cause and end my career.

In a war zone, the DISCOM commander was giving me an hour of his time. That is a long time. One would think my quality control must have been catastrophic to get that much time to talk about it, so I had to make his hour worthwhile. I chuckled.

Whether their crazed fear was coming from the possibility of me making general twenty years from then or not, this was cruel, insensitive, and abusive.

Sitting at my desk, I didn't know what to do. I needed slides—slides in the desert! My company did not have access to a projector, so I wouldn't have slides. Of course, McAfee from the battalion staff didn't offer slides, guidance, nor assistance. They have set me up to fail with an almost insurmountable task attempting to trip me up. I have to figure out how to beat them.

I was so tired, and I had not had a complete night's sleep since my dad died. It is just part of grieving. I would wake up frequently during the night and lie there, tired but unable to sleep.

Feeling the cumulative weight of their betrayal, my grief, remaining a positive upbeat leader of my unit, and standing up for myself, I placed my head on my desk to meditate.

I hated having to tell my officers about this. I kept my people above the racial nonsense spewing from battalion because it could disrupt my company, and I would not have that. I discussed everything with my first sergeant except what I perceived as problems caused by discrimination against me. I respected my first sergeant; we had a wonderful relationship and planned to keep it that way. We didn't have racial issues in my company which is almost evenly divided into one-third Latino, one-third Black and one-third White.

Composed, after a few minutes, I briefed my first sergeant on my task to brief the DISCOM commander. First, I needed briefing slides and markers. I asked the first sergeant to ask Sergeant Howard, our supply sergeant, if she could find me one hundred slides and a box of permanent markers. I couldn't do anything without those materials.

Within an hour, Sergeant Howard placed two boxes of slides and a box of markers on my desk.

I laughed out loud and clapped my hands all while asking her where she had gotten them. She laughed and said something like, "A good officer never asks the supply sergeant a question like that," then said that she brought them just in case.

Leaving my office area, Sergeant Howard said laughing, "Let me know if you need anything else, Ma'am."

I thanked her, knowing I couldn't make it without her. She always came through. She was awesome! She had a slight smile, lifting one side of her face, when she accomplished the impossible. She left with that look on her face.

Planning backward, I needed to be ready to brief for sixty minutes at 1800 hours tomorrow in order to set up, check the equipment, practice, and relax before the briefing starts.

I needed an approach to the briefing that would last an hour but answer all possible issues related to customer service.

Scrolling through my desk top briefing I got an idea—if the DISCOM commander wanted a briefing, I would give him a briefing! No one knew this company better than me.

Using my field phone, I told Lieutenant Hemsley to come to my office with Warrant Officer Four Clarkston, the chief maintenance quality control technician, and Warrant Officer Three Alando, the chief mechanical and automotive maintenance technician. My three officers were there within ten minutes.

I was forced to tell them about the task McAfee brought me from the DISCOM commander. They had questions, but I kept them focused.

I needed data—correct data—as soon as possible, and I knew these three men would get it for me.

First, I needed to know if we had customer complaints I didn't know about. I was assured there had been no customer complaints made to our Shop Office.

I shared Major McAfee said there had been customer complaints sufficient to justify the task I'd received suggesting maybe the complaints were to Major McAfee's staff in Support Operations rather than to our Shop Office.

The chiefs explained that was unlikely because Support Operations collects data and reports that didn't give him visibility of our operations in that way. I nodded my head in agreement. Still confused and questioning what was causing me to brief the DISCOM commander, the three officers talked among themselves until I interrupted.

"Mr. Clarkston, quality control is your lane; I am not the quality control officer. The complaint is against you and your shop. I am briefing, but the complaint questions your work."

Chief Clarkston, a proud gentleman, was rightfully offended. He said, "Ma'am, I don't know what this is about. We have not had any customer complaints, and I will tell that to Major McAfee and anybody else."

Shaking my head in agreement, "I believe what you are saying chief; all our computer data supports you. We will all find out what is happening tomorrow night. My briefing gives me the opportunity to defend your work, our work, our shops and contact teams, and our company."

Mr. Clarkston, getting a little testy, blurted, "Ma'am, what is this all about?"

I answered so everyone can hear, "You know as much as I know. To say more would only be speculation, and what good does that do us? Let's stay focused. They want a briefing, so we are going to give them a briefing. *Hooah*! This is what I need."

I passed out assignments to my officers. Each one had different tasks. "I need your input today not later than 2100 hours. Sooner is better guys, but don't be late. Any questions?"

They responded, "Got it, Ma'am."

As they left, I heard Lieutenant Hemsley whisper to Chief Clarkston in his strong Tennessee accent, "Ain't this some shit, chief? What are they trying to do?"

I couldn't hear Mr. Clarkston's response, but I knew he was not happy.

Chief Alando stayed back to talk. He was like that—always looking out for me. I admired him so much. He knew every Army regulation, manual, and publication by name and paragraph number. He was a professional, a walking library—the best officer I had ever worked with.

Chewing gum, Chief Alando said, "Captain Davis, do you need anything else? Do you want help making slides?"

I responded confidently, "I have it chief. I know what I am going to do. The data you, the lieutenant, and Chief Clarkston are putting together will be the most important part of the briefing. Help them get it to me."

Mr. Alando said, "You can count on me, Ma'am. See you later."

I responded, "I know I can. Thanks, chief. You guys are what get me through."

Mr. Alando left to help collect and verify the data; I conceptualized my plan and outlined my briefing.

I started formatting the brief—first introduce myself, "Good Evening Sir … I am Captain Davis, commander of … The purpose of the briefing is to update you on current status of …"

I stopped as the first sergeant looked in, "Ma'am, do you have everything you need?"

I responded, "I don't need a thing. Thank you, first sergeant. What is going on … is everything okay?"

The first sergeant said, "Nothing for you to be concerned about Ma'am. I will keep the generator running for you, and know that no one will bother you until you say so. Let me know if you need anything."

"Thanks first sergeant, I appreciate your help." I responded looking back down at the papers on my desk.

Before sundown, Lieutenant Hemsley and the chiefs brought back data collected for me. I had everything I needed, but manually preparing an hour-long briefing took time.

I decided to brief the entire company from its structure to the last piece of customer equipment work ordered and received through quality control. I worked through the night, not getting a wink of sleep, making slide after slide, pausing to reflect, citing references, and drawing illustrations, flow charts, and graphics. I broke my presentation into five parts capturing everything the company was—personnel and equipment; work areas, shops, and unit readiness rate; our current present tactical location and security plan; what we did, maintenance operations—using flow charts and graphics. I finally ended with the rate of customer equipment returned due to poor quality control.

The company completed almost one thousand work orders within 2.5 months of operation in Saudi. That is phenomenal considering we fixed every item in the division inventory except missiles and aviation equipment. I was so very proud of our statistics. My troops should have been getting accolades for their work instead of supposed complaints.

I stayed up all night, and by noon, eighty-three slides were ready for first review and correction. Moving on adrenaline, I was so hyped I couldn't eat, and even though I felt hollow and exhausted, I was not sleepy.

I dragged myself up to my quarters for personal hygiene before starting to practice the presentation and performing slide modifications and deletions. I anticipated a call from my battalion commander, but so far, he hadn't made contact with me, not even to wish me luck. He clearly didn't care about me, but I didn't need him; I was fearless!

Afternoon passed quickly, and after three practices and numerous corrections, I was ready. My driver brought my vehicle for my trip to DISCOM Headquarters which took just under an hour. My shop officer and warrant officers, who were accompanying me to the briefing, traveled together in a separate vehicle. I preferred the quiet of driving alone.

In no time I passed through the DISCOM checkpoint. It was dark so I followed the light of meticulously laid chemical lights that guided me through a maze of Army vehicles to DISCOM briefing tents leading to DISCOM Headquarters. I paused to relax a few minutes, just to take a breath before getting directions to the briefing tent. Inside, a bright white light shined circularly, lighting the tent from the center out. The projector was under the light pole facing the screen. My lieutenant would be my slides changer, so we rehearsed a few slides to synchronize our effort. I welcomed the silence when my lieutenant and chiefs visited the Division Materiel Management Center commodity managers.

About twenty minutes to the hour, my officers entered the tent followed by six commodity officers. My friend Marilynn was amongst the group. Soon after, principal members of the DISCOM commander's staff including the DISCOM command sergeant major filtered in, and some officers I didn't recognize took a seat. Finally, just minutes before briefing time, my battalion commander and his staff—including his command sergeant major—took their seats. When, I saw McAfee, a confidence radiated inside me from head to toe. I told him this wouldn't work …

The tent was full to capacity, approximately thirty seats. I didn't speak to anyone, and no one spoke to me. A few seconds before 2000 hours everyone was quiet. They knew what would happen next, and I think they were prepared to do their part. My officers were seated next to me on the front row.

The DISCOM command sergeant major standing at the door called the tent to attention and announced the commander as he entered. Everyone stood.

He said, "Take your seats; take your seats."

I took my position up front. Lieutenant Hemsley was watching me.

The DISCOM commander said, "Okay. Are we ready?"

I answered, "Yes, Sir!" With my pointer in my right hand, I started my introduction. Over the next two slides, I stated the purpose of the briefing as the commander nodded his head.

At about the fourth slide, the DISCOM commander had a question.

I responded, "Yes, Sir, I have that later in the briefing, but if you would like for me to go forward, I can brief it now."

He said, "No that is all right. I will wait."

I continued, and the DISCOM commander asked another question.

I answered, "Yes Sir, I cover that in the next two slides. Next slide." The slide answered his question.

He nodded … I said, "Next slide," and explained its content.

The DISCOM commander asked another question, but before I could speak, he said "I guess you will answer this question later in your briefing?"

I answered, "Yes, Sir."

He said, "Okay, go ahead." Afterward there were no more questions.

Using the skills developed by observing master briefers in my other assignments … that night, I was the master. I briefed using my pointer without moving my feet. My head faced straight ahead—never turning to look at the screen behind me, remaining in the modified "at ease" position. My left arm was loose at my side as I move through the briefing without notes.

I could see the faces of people on the front row; all others were shadows. The room was silent.

I finally got to the slide showing returned items work-ordered for repeat maintenance out of about one thousand work orders complete. I explained, "Sir, two radios were returned for repeat or corrective maintenance." And I presented details of the repair deficiencies and the dates of initial repair, of the corrected repair and when the items were returned to our customers.

Everyone was quiet.

I paused … before going to my summary statement. Hemsley flipped the final slide that had one word, "Questions?"

I said, "Subject to your questions, Sir, this concludes my briefing." The briefing took just over sixty minutes. Someone turned the lights on; now I could see their faces.

The DISCOM commander shook his head from side to side in disbelief, "That was one excellent briefing." He paused, grimacing his lips, and shook his head again speaking louder, "one excellent briefing." I maintained my modified "at ease" stance, the tip of my pointer now touching the ground, both arms along my sides, my feet spread apart pressed into the dirt; my breaths were shallow.

The DISCOM commander, turned in his seat looking at the crowd to his right, "Are there any questions?" Then to his left side where my battalion commander and staff were seated, "Any questions?"

My battalion commander looked at the floor; his command sergeant major and staff were all looking away from me. The tent was silent. Captain Greyson was sitting on the back row next to Marilynn.

As I stood there, moving only my eyes to look around the tent, I felt small like a pebble, or even invisible. I just stood, frozen facing their obvious contempt for me.

The DISCOM commander said, "That was an excellent job."

He addressed the room, "That is the best company briefing I have ever had. We need to have other company commanders to give this same briefing." He turned to his executive officer, "XO, schedule some of the other company commanders to brief me."

The executive officer responded, "Yes Sir … Yes Sir."

Who did they think they were fooling? No other company commanders would be made to do this. He said that because their actions were—by legal definition—disparate treatment, by race and possibly also gender.

The DISCOM commander's comments didn't change the facts. This briefing was a singular hateful event planned to denigrate me and relieve me from command. The DISCOM had three forward battalions that contained four companies each, and not one of those commanders had to brief. My battalion had six companies; was I the only commander of concern? Not hardly, I had the best company in DISCOM, and I knew it. Now, thanks to this briefing the new DISCOM commander knew it too, and so did his guests.

Yep, this was a party setup to kill my command and my career. I was told I would be briefing the DISCOM commander, yet a room full of logisticians showed up. I could only assume that in their scenario, I was supposed to have fallen under the pressure of a barrage of unanswerable questions … coming from the powerful group of logistics intellectuals who knew how to intimidate someone like me. I assume the DISCOM commander in outrage because of my inadequacy would have no choice but to relieve me of command and, for the good of the Army, replace me with Captain Greyson. Greyson would then travel to my company, rally the troops, and provide the competent leadership needed. My battalion commander would announce to my troops that I would not be back. I would be cast aside somewhere until my career ended because I had been relieved and couldn't get promoted. Then in DISCOM all would be white (I mean right) in their world.

Like a pack of wild dogs, their strength lay in their numbers. An individual wild dog might get his butt beat in a fight, but a pack of wild dogs attack and cover for each other until they kill their prey. That night, in that tent, they showed their strength, and I showed mine. They were vicious, but I was victorious.

Their bullying and dirty fighting had gone too far. I honestly think they believed their right to the Army and this country was greater than mine. And to that I say, think what you want, but don't act on it, because your rights end where mine begin. That night, they trampled on both my rights and my spirit. I could do nothing about it, but I refused to hate them as they hated me because I was above that.

I wondered why the DISCOM commander let it happen. His responsibility was to stop it, but instead he supported it. Their harsh and mean treatment had eroded my confidence in their leadership abilities … and I was supposed to go into combat with these people!

The DISCOM commander looked at me, "Good job, good job, very good job."

I thanked him. The command sergeant major called the room to attention. The commander left, and others filtered out behind him. My battalion commander and his staff disappeared without a word to me. And just like a puff of smoke, their outrageous treatment of me was dissolved, vanished, unimportant, and forgotten by everyone except me. I hurt.

People talked to each other while milling around as they did after staff meetings. From the back row, Marilynn smiled as she waved good-bye.

My officers stood, whispering to each other, looking around until the tent was empty. I was in the same spot, numb—almost to the point of lifelessness.

I moved, and the accolades began from my officers. I didn't know who said what, but among the comments were:

"Woo-wee, Ma'am, you blew them away."

"I am so proud of you Captain Davis."

"They couldn't say nothing …"

"You were great!"

I remember it was Mr. Clarkston who said, "I started to ask them why you had to brief? It doesn't make sense!"

I shook my head in agreement, but I think my officers had enough information to draw conclusions without my input.

"Yeah," Lieutenant Hemsley chimed in, "What caused this? Why you?"

I couldn't say anything because there was nothing left.

Mr. Alando said, "You did it and I mean you really did it, they will not bother you again, Captain Davis. Not one of them had anything to say."

The lieutenant added, "Ma'am, you never looked back, just kept on talking and pointing, woo-wee, like a machine! They couldn't touch you, Ma'am."

Smiling, I thanked Lieutenant Hemsley for flipping the slides; I told him he was perfect.

After collecting our things, we left the tent together. Someone asked if I wanted company on my ride back, but I declined the offer, explaining I needed time to deescalate.

Driving back, I thought of my family. My daddy would be proud of me tonight, and I was proud to have the name Davis on my shirt. Those men in my battalion and the DISCOM commander were not of my kind. I could never have treated a subordinate the way they treated me. They were monsters, but I faced them without fear. They attacked me, I took a stand, and my faith pulled me through.

When I got to my tent I went straight to sleep.

A few days later, in the afternoon, the DISCOM commander's vehicle drove through my company area. I went out to greet him, but he stated he was just looking around and would not get out of his vehicle.

Again, he told me I was doing a really good job and commended my briefing. It seemed as if he was apologizing, so I thanked him.

Mumbling he said, "I still have a lot of other great captains, who are waiting for command, too, but you are doing a very good job."

I thanked him again. I stood cheekbones high, and remained polite and cordial, but inside I didn't respect him. To me he is racist; what is there for me to like? I watched his vehicle as it drove away and disappeared behind a sand dune.

I wonder why he told me, "He has other great captains who are waiting for command." Should I give up my command to one of his other great captains? "No!"

The DISCOM commander showed no shamed when he spoke to me, but what happened in his briefing tent was disgraceful and beneath the dignity of his position. It was discriminatory and racist, and he allowed it. To me, it was disgusting, and he was disgusting. I had a bad taste in my mouth, took a sip of water, and spat.

CHAPTER 9

THANK YOU FOR THE TRUTH

———

"What about that, another soldier with marijuana, first sergeant?" I asked.

A hookah pipe with marijuana residue was found in the possession of Specialist Four Rose, a soldier who worked in one of the company's maintenance teams located miles forward of the company main area.

My first sergeant warned me that Rose was in the company Orderly Room waiting to be picked up by military police.

I recalled one of my privates was accused of having marijuana a few weeks before, but none was found. Now, marijuana was found on Rose. Maybe someone did successfully smuggle contraband into theater and into my company, and that might explained things. I mean that would have made sense if the first group of military police confused the private with Rose, who was the real culprit.

Rose stood at attention and greeted me as I walked through the Orderly Room to my office in the back of the tent.

The first sergeant was out when two military policemen entered the Orderly Room tent to arrest Specialist Rose, so I came out of my office to witness his apprehension. For clarity I asked the military police sergeant what crime was committed.

He explained, "Specialist Rose is in possession of a pipe which contains residual marijuana."

Wondering I ask, "How did the military police find out Specialist Rose had a pipe?"

The military policeman said, "My headquarters told us."

My curiosity was peaked so I asked, "Who told your headquarters that Specialist Rose had a pipe and marijuana?"

The military police sergeant was not making sense. Rose was in a team of my mechanics that worked and lived together under the charge of a noncommissioned officer from my company. The team was collocated with our customer unit, but my noncommissioned officers oversaw my soldiers. No one should have had access to Rose and his personal belongings without interaction with his noncommissioned officer.

So how did the military police find a pipe and marijuana in Rose's personal gear without involving my company's noncommissioned officer in charge of that site?

I asked, "Who reported Specialist Rose to the police for possession? Was it his noncommissioned officer?"

The policeman said he didn't know who reported Rose, but he had orders to take him in.

I responded, "I am not going to release this soldier without a clear understanding of his offense. I am sorry sergeant, but something isn't right here. I need to know why this soldier is under arrest."

The military police sergeant was upset. "Ma'am, he is clearly in possession of illegal paraphernalia. You are interfering with official police business." He paused then added, "You should talk with your battalion commander because he knows what is going on." He waited for my reaction then added, "I am going to report you to your battalion commander for interfering with my duty to arrest this soldier."

I was not moved by the sergeant's comments and authority because I believed Rose had been set up. I wouldn't let him go because once arrested, I couldn't control what happened to him; so, he had to stay until I found out the truth.

Also, the sergeant had said the magic words, "battalion commander". I wanted to know what the battalion commander knew about Rose that I didn't.

"Sergeant I am not trying to give you a hard time, and I don't want to stop you from doing your duty but nothing you've said makes sense, so I am not releasing this soldier."

The military policemen reluctantly left the tent and got into their vehicle. I could hear them make radio calls to someone.

At any moment I expected to hear from my battalion commander, while I sat with Rose in the Orderly Room. A large pipe was clearly visible inside the specialist's open duffel bag. I was suspicious.

I asked Rose, "Is this your pipe?"

He said, "Yes, Ma'am."

"How did you get that pipe into theater? Where did you get marijuana?"

He couldn't explain how a pipe which stands about three feet in height got through numerous unit inspections at Fort Hood and through customs in Europe and Saudi Arabia. The pipe all but consumed his duffel bag without other items. Without any doubt that pipe would have been seen and confiscated.

The company's noncommissioned officers conducted numerous unit inspections multiple times to ensure soldiers packed the gear needed for survival in combat. Items in our mandatory military packing list took up every bit of space in the two duffel bags each soldier carried from the United States.

I pushed Rose to explain where the pipe came from; he couldn't explain it, so I went back to work in my office.

After about fifteen minutes, Rose knocked on the canvas separating my office from the Orderly Room and entered. He wanted to talk, so I told him to have a seat.

Rose started talking, "Ma'am thank you for stopping them from arresting me. You are a great commander, and I appreciate what you did."

He made some more positive comments about me as his commander, and the unit.

"I would do the same for anyone in our unit, Rose, when I know something is not right."

He moves about in his chair, "I know you are looking out for me, but I am asking you to let the military police take me."

Surprised I asked, "Why would I let them do that? I know you didn't bring a pipe in your duffel bag from the United States, I know you have not received a pipe in the mail, and I know you didn't smoke marijuana in the vicinity of the maintenance team."

After a few seconds he answered, "I am going to trust you Ma'am, so … I am going to tell you something that if you repeat it, I will be in trouble."

"Rose, I can't promise to help you hide a crime, anything illegal, unethical, dangerous, unsafe, or immoral."

Rose said, "No Ma'am, nothing like that."

He paused. I watched him as he searched for the right words then said, "I believe I can trust you Ma'am, so I am going to trust you … I was placed in your company to cause disruption among the soldiers. Something has happened in another unit, I am needed there, so I have to leave. Do you understand? You need to let me go."

I'm flabbergasted, "Are you kidding? You were placed here to disrupt the unit? Who did that, who put you in this company?"

Rose responded calmly, "I don't have all of the details, but the battalion commander knows everything. He knows why I am here and that I am leaving."

"Specialist Rose, I believe you, and I promise to protect your confidence. You have opened my eyes. Thank you for telling me this. I was fighting for you because I knew something was wrong with that arrest. I thought you were being trapped by the police, but I see, the pipe was staged to have you arrested. I understand, and I will let them take you."

Rose said, "Trust me Ma'am, you have a good unit. They love you, and anyone can see that you love them; I had fun."

"Thank you, Specialist Rose. You guys are the Army's best; you pushed me to be better. I enjoyed having you in this company, and I hate to see you go. Again, thank you for telling me the truth. I appreciate it."

Rose and I exchanged mutual words of respect. When we heard the first sergeant on the other side of the tent Rose stood, saluted, and left my office.

I sat back in my chair. My battalion commander had surprised me yet again. This guy just wouldn't stop. I thought he couldn't surprise me again, but he did, and I had never heard anything worse than this. He placed a saboteur in my company to disrupt it. I didn't know the Army let people place spies and saboteurs inside their own units. What was his probable cause? I guess probable cause wasn't needed to disrupt a unit. But disrupting a unit contradicts and disrespects the entire chain of discipline.

My mind was racing to remember the many strange and unexplainable occurrences that took place while Rose was in the company. My private had to dump his gear out to prove he didn't have drugs, and a lieutenant refused to follow my directive because he thought it was stupid. And the warrant officers refusing deployment—was that part of commander's plan to disrupt the company? I wondered if the battalion commander put them up to complaining. He was slick and calculating … just enough to ask the chiefs to do something like that. Who knows? And oh, my goodness, I wonder how many disturbances were staged by Rose that caused some other soldiers to have been undeservedly disciplined. I really hoped that didn't happen, and it should not have because checks were in place to prevent abuse through discipline. I should have asked Rose about that … but no, no I shouldn't have because he has told me enough. I was now wise to the dealings of my battalion commander. A hateful man lies behind his smile and pleasant voice.

I was distracted by movement in the outer office then by a man's voice, "First sergeant, we are here to take charge of Specialist Rose."

I heard more scuffling about as Specialist Rose was escorted out of the tent. *Farewell and best wishes, Specialist Rose, and thank you for the truth.*

One evening, I had been in my office all day. Rose had given me a new perspective, another piece of the puzzle the commander had devised. Rose was in the company for a long time, whatever his purpose and whatever his disruptions, we all made it through, and before he left, he gave me his trust.

I didn't know what to expect from my chain of command, and at that point I didn't put anything past them. I stayed in prayer and renewed my mind by reading the Word of God. When looking at me they see a skinny Black woman, but I am so much more.

Another day was ending, and with that came hope of a better tomorrow. The generator was off for the night, so I lay in my sleeping bag lighted by my flashlight reading from the King James version of the Bible.

Psalms 91. *"I will say of the Lord, He is my refuge and my fortress: my God, in him will I trust. Surely, he shall deliver thee from the snare of the fowler and from the noisome pestilence. He shall cover thee with his feathers, and under his wings shalt thou trust: his truth shall be thy shield and buckler. Thou shalt not be afraid for the terror by night, nor for the arrow that flieth by day, nor for the pestilence that walketh in darkness, nor for the destruction that wasteth at noonday … Because thou hast made the Lord, which is my refuge, even the most High, thy habitation; There shall no evil befall thee …"*

I was exhausted. Being around the people in that battalion was like running hurdles, jump after jump without rest in between. Each jump had to be perfect, in a never-ending race; I must be perfect, in every way, at all times because they have set traps. I was tired, so tired; I drifted into sound sleep.

CHAPTER 10

COMMUNICATIONS CHECK

———

Tap, tap, tap, tap, tap … I heard tapping on my tent.

It was the first sergeant, "Ma'am, battalion is up to their same old stuff; they are saying we didn't connect our landline to the battalion command center, but Specialist Curtis told me he connected us as soon as we arrived. He logged the communications check three hours ago. I told that to those guys, but the battalion commander wants to meet with you in fifteen minutes."

At sunrise, I was recovering from our exhausting overnight move to a location that positioned us closer to our customer units. It was a cool morning, so I lay on my cot wearing my sweater and field jack.

I responded, "This must be a mistake first sergeant; I'll take care of it. Thanks, first sergeant."

Really! The battalion commander wanted to talk about a late communications line. We certainly should have connected into battalion, but was this cause for discussion at command level? From experience, a call from the battalion commander to me was always bad news. I suspected he was attempting to berate my troops. The first sergeant thought so too, and that was why he said they were up to their old stuff.

I saw the commander coming in the distance as I drove to a spot abutting my company perimeter with that of the battalion headquarters. I respected his rank and position, but my respect for the man had long gone. I remembered the hooded racist terrorists that use to march in Raleigh when I was a little child. He represented what I thought they looked like under their hoods. His fight with me seemed personal, malicious, and bazaar. I have not known hatred like this … it was unnatural.

I drove to where he stopped and got out of my vehicle, saluted, and walked to the hood of his vehicle. We leaned on the vehicle like two buddies chatting about good times. He started to talk about the disconnected landline. I listened, but I believe he knows the communications check was performed. I viewed this as another harassment tactic—an antic, to call me on the carpet.

When he finished, I offered my Charge of Quarters log for review, "Sir, as you can see the landline communications check was annotated by my communications specialist hours ago. I believe my specialist checked my landline at that time. Either someone at Battalion Headquarters left our communication check off your log or my communications specialist is lying, and, Sir, my specialist isn't lying. His performance is always exceptional in both our communications maintenance shop and in support of the company. As a precaution he is backtracking his work to find any flaw in our connection but that doesn't change the fact that he made a communications check with battalion hours ago; perhaps the problem is in the command operations center."

The commander was defensive, "No one in Headquarters has a reason to falsify the log."

I answered, "I agree, Sir, no one had a reason to do it, but that doesn't mean they didn't do it. No one has a reason to do anything against me and this company. In general, we are hard workers trying to do our jobs to the highest military standards and to the best of our abilities; I am speaking for everyone in this company, from my youngest private to me. You know my company is well disciplined and performs consistently to highest standards."

He agreed with me, shaking his head.

"Sir, I will not tolerate the way people are treating my officers and my troops. Specialist Curtis is frustrated this morning because he takes pride in his work, and he knows a communications check was made last night. Curtis doesn't deserve this frustration.

"Also, Sir I want to ask you about this. I was told that while I was at home for my dad's funeral, a field-grade officer Major McAfee called Lieutenant Hemsley—my company's acting commander—an A-hole while in staff meeting. With all due respect, Sir, if that happened, why did you allow that to happen? Why? Neither my lieutenants nor any officer deserves to be demeaned in that way. It was wrong, disrespectful, and I found it offensive because when people curse my lieutenant, they curse me. My lieutenants speak for me. Any problems with my lieutenants should be addressed to me. With all due respect, Sir, at this point I don't put anything beneath your staff. There seems to be no limit to the unhinged animus towards me and the innocent people assigned to my company. Sir, I want you to know that while on emergency leave and in subsequent letters, I have told my family what is happening and to look for you if something happens to me. I told my mother to look for you because you will know what and why it happened." The words rolled freely out of my mouth.

Surprised he responded, "You mean … Cleo, you think I would harm you?"

"Yes, Sir, I do."

Gesturing one hand open to the sky he said, "Why? Why do you think that?"

Actually, I had enough of this fake guy, but I kept my bearing. Cheekbones high, I said, "Why, Sir, did I have to brief the DISCOM commander on the status of my company? Why did that happen? So, why was I the only commander in the DISCOM selected to brief the colonel? You know I have a desk top briefing, so why was the hour-long briefing mandatory, on viewgraph projector slides? Everyone knows company commanders are not authorized a viewgraph, so why would anyone expect that I would have sufficient slides for a one-hour briefing, in a combat zone? To do that briefing was all but impossible to do, but no one stopped it. Why? And Sir, with all due respect, you are here today to talk about a communications wire, but I neither heard from you before I was to brief, nor after the briefing. Customer complaints about quality control were proved to be untrue. Sir, why did that briefing happen? I saw you and your staff at the briefing; what was that all about? Did you arrange the briefing Sir, if so, why? So many questions, Sir. So many whys. So many questions without reasons and answers."

He didn't say anything.

I continued, "Sir, a friend in Division Headquarters, told me that you and the DISCOM commander, petitioned the assistant division commander support to remove me from command while I was on leave for my dad's funeral. If you did that, why? The obsession with me in command is why my family will look at American troops before Iraqi forces if something happens to me."

Guessing, I asked, "Why did you have Staff Sergeant Christy tell me that she is homosexual? Was it to find out if I am homosexual? Well, I am not. I am heterosexual, but more importantly I am human, Sir. With all due respect, I want you to know that I am human. When you stress one of my privates by having him searched for drugs, you stress all of his tent mates and his noncommissioned officers thereby adding unnecessary duress on the unit. Why would any professional soldier do that to a unit under any conditions but especially now under these conditions, in a foreign country preparing to face our country's enemy?"

When he didn't respond, I kept going. "I wonder, Sir, why the hatred for me? I am a woman, a lady, a daughter; I have feelings. I am flesh and blood; my heart beats and blood flows through my body. Why is so much energy expended to keep me in a place beneath humanity. Please Sir, please don't forget that I am human because once you reduce me to something less than a human being, any atrocity will seem justified." I lower my head.

"This communications check is just another … thing to upset my troops. Curtis is upset because he feels he let the first sergeant and the unit down. My soldiers and first sergeant are people, like other soldiers. They shouldn't be punished because they are in my unit."

I paused.

"But that is okay, Sir. I am responsible for leadership in this unit, and we will adjust to keep spirits high because we need soldiers at their best as we progress toward Deployment Day (D-Day). I just ask that you stop external sources who are designated to cause disturbances in my company. Please Sir, stop them."

He said, "Well Cleo, I will do everything I can to stop all harassment and disrespect shown to you and your troops. I will not let anyone in this battalion harm you; I don't want you to feel that anyone would. I would never let that happen."

I listened and nodded in agreement, but I didn't feel anything. To me, he was a sneaky liar.

But I responded, "Thank you Sir, I appreciate that."

Then our conversation evolved. He acknowledged the great job I did briefing the DISCOM commander, and he conceded that discipline and excellence are obvious in my company.

As he spoke, I remembered him calling me in for counseling before sixty days in command to tell me to ease up on the unit, comparing me to Humphrey Bogart, in the movie, *The Caine Mutiny*. If I had listened, the company wouldn't have been ready to deploy, and I would have been relieved for cause. And I remembered he was negotiating conditions to remove me from command while I was on emergency leave for the death of my parent! I believe he planned for the gallery of senior logistics officers to attack my briefing and bombard me with questions I couldn't answer. He planned to let the DISCOM commander relieve me and to replace me with Captain Greyson … for no other reason but because he is a White man. I know he maintained communication with my predecessor and some of my warrant officers in the attempt to find weaknesses in my command and undermine my authority, but worst of all, I know he placed an agent in my unit to create conflict amongst my troops, and for that alone, he is dirt.

I accepted what he said because we had a real war to fight, and we were not enemies.

Taking a breath I said, "Thank you Sir, I will remember your promise. I needed to know that you will not compromise the lives of my soldiers because you want to harm me."

The tone of our conversation became pleasant before we bid each other farewell.

When I got back to the unit, all modes of communication were operational, and we had a successful communications check. The incident was not mentioned again.

I went on about the numerous tasks associated with commanding.

Christmas was nearing and for many of my young soldiers this would be their first Christmas away from home. Some were high school students a year ago; now they were in combat defending their country. My supply sergeant, Sergeant Howard overheard some of the younger soldiers saying this would be the worst Christmas ever, so her supply section wrapped everyone a gift of Army socks and T-shirts. Everyone needed what they got. What a great idea! She was so thoughtful and smart, a great noncommissioned officer and wonderful person. I admired my soldiers and had empathy for those who were missing Mama, home, Christmas trees, gifts, lights, even holiday music. Equally, I respected their sacrifice. They were gladiators standing between their country's success or defeat.

Lying on my cot in darkness later that evening I was thankful to have survived another day. I reflected on my years of emotional abuse and racially motivated obstacles I had survived while in the Army. For me, the arch of racism in America is magnified in the Army. There is no safe space, no vehicle for change; the hateful environment flows just below the surface from job to job, unit to unit. I once thought hard work and exceptionalism would change minds and thereby eventually fade prejudices and injustice. Now, I accept that I was living within an institution of systemic abuse—a form of tyranny for which the Army offers no redress of grievances because publicly racial discrimination, abuse, and oppression did not exist.

CHAPTER 11

LINE OF DEPARTURE

Captain Cleola Davis, Company Commander, Desert Shield/
Desert Storm 1990.

"Boom … boom." I heard what was like distant artillery fire. This was January 17, 1991; United States and coalition forces combat operations had begun in Iraq.

I looked at my watch in my sleeping bag; it was after midnight.

I had a map, torn from the front page of a newspaper, showing the general location of all United States Army divisions. My division was near the city Hafar al-Batin in northern Saudi Arabia, near Iraq.

"Boom … boom … boom, boom." The rhythm continued periodically at night for a few weeks until I couldn't hear it anymore.

In late February, the battalion commander briefed our movement order. The plan was to move the hundreds of vehicles and trailers assigned to DISCOM Headquarters, the Materiel Management Center, and my battalion in one linear, bumper-to-bumper march unit across the desert into Iraq.

My company owned five to seven tracked vehicles used as maintenance reserves to exchange one for one with combat units when they required immediate equipment replacement to stay in the fight. My tracked vehicles and two tracked vehicles from a chemical company moved in a convoy together along a separate route engineered to support tanks and other tracked vehicles. The battalion operations officer, Captain Jason, oversaw their movement.

I was fortunate to get new personnel about two months prior that brought my unit to over 100 percent of its authorized strength. I was very happy to get a master sergeant who, while unauthorized, was a great asset. My first sergeant was happy too, to have a person of equal rank who could help with his work. During this movement the first sergeant placed Master Sergeant Mathews in charge of our tracks and crews.

After the battalion movement briefing, I met my officers to back brief them and held a final company meeting before going into combat.

The first sergeant formed the unit in a semicircle before I took charge. Seated together, everyone looked calm and ready. I shared what was on my heart because it seemed right.

"We are a strong unit; you are strong individuals; each individual is at his and her best. You are ready; we are ready. We are trained and ready to perform our mission, and you will do it. The units we support are depending on us, and the members of our company who are supporting forward units are already in Iraq. It is our duty to join them and to back them up. We will all be together again when we free Kuwait and complete our duty to our country. Are there any questions?"

Nobody had questions, so I reiterated skills they already knew: stay alert, keep a buddy at all times, maintain your bearing and discipline, look out for each other and don't take chances, stay on the movement route, don't walk off the route and don't touch anything on the ground, and be prepared to engage enemy forces.

I stated, "We are going into their country, onto their terrain. We are soldiers, and we will do what soldiers do to defend ourselves, our brothers, and our country."

Before releasing them to the first sergeant, I closed, "I am proud to be your commander; you are the best. I don't know if you believe in God, but I do, and I want you to know I pray for each one of you by name … you are in my prayers. Okay, we are ready; this is what we are trained to do. I am fired up, and you are fired up. Take care of each other, *Hooah!* Raise up maintenance! Company attention! First sergeant!"

I walked away as the noncommissioned officers and lieutenants took charge.

As dusk fell, our battalion vehicles were intermingled with those of DISCOM Headquarters, and the huge Materiel Management Center vehicles forming an endless sluggishly lumbering convoy. We were moving under radio listening silence, which means we only spoke in an emergency.

Hundreds of large supply trucks—the size of commercial 18-wheel trucks—moving forward between 5-ton trucks, 2 ½ ton vans, and Humvees resembled medieval dragons creeping along the flat grey sand.

As hours passed, the gentle roar of my vehicles engine and intermittent stopping for periods lasting minutes at a time made me sleepy, but my driver appeared awake and alert.

"Help! Help! I'm lost, I'm lost!" Out of nowhere a woman's voice was screaming on the radio.

I was concerned, but since I didn't have any female soldiers with access to a radio, I listened for others to react.

My battalion commander used his call sign to respond, "Who are you? Over."

Another person using his call sign echoes my battalion commander, "What is your call sign? Over."

Panicked and yelling, she used her call sign which identified her as a captain assigned to DISCOM Headquarters. She stated some trucks were behind her vehicle, but nothing was visible to her front. Mixing multiple unit vehicles in a single linear convoy with no check points, and no sequence list of vehicles by bumper number, had come back to haunt our movement planners because we had no way to identify where she was in march sequence. Glancing left at my driver, I became aware that other privates and soldiers riding in vehicles with radios on this frequency could hear her cry for help.

Someone said, "Where are you? Over."

The captain screamed, "I don't know!"

A male voice responded, "Do you have a map? Over."

The captain replied, "Yes."

A male voice spoke, "We need to know your location. Over."

Everyone was quiet.

Breaking silence, the captain gave an eight-digit grid coordinate. Unfolding my map to locate the point she identified, I hoped the enemy wasn't monitoring our radio frequency because they could attack her position. But when I found the point, I laughed because it was in Iraq. She had not had enough time to reach that location.

My battalion commander used his call sign. "Are you sure of your location? Over."

She responded, "I don't know; I don't know!"

No one knew where she was located; the radio was silent again.

I wondered, *Is she in front of me ... or is she behind my vehicle?* If she was behind me, she only needed to move forward, but if she was ahead, we may have all been lost.

I figured, we were moving before she cried out, so she must have been behind me. I don't remember how I figured that out, but using my radio call sign I asked the battalion commander for permission to leave the convoy in search of the missing officer and vehicles. The commander asked if I knew where she was located. I replied "no," but I thought she was behind me. He granted me permission to search for her.

My driver and I passed convoy vehicles from 18-wheelers to Humvees, standing in line waiting to move until finally, there was a break in the convoy. Following deep grooves cut in the sand, we tracked backward for about ten minutes until silhouettes of big rectangular boxes were visible. My driver spotted them and drove to their location. Somehow the captain and the vehicles immediately behind her were completely disconnected from the main convoy.

I was very happy to radio to my commander, "We have found the vehicles. More to follow, over."

He responded, "Roger, over."

Approaching the captain's vehicle, from the rear I told my driver to stop, giving me some distance to speak with the captain privately.

I sprang out of my door, moving fast toward her as she walked toward me talking about being lost. She was excited and seemed frustrated.

Out of earshot of our soldiers, I told her, "Calm down."

She continued to talk.

Again, in a stronger tone I said, "Calm down. Calm down."

She was still talking. I tried to calm her down.

"Captain, please … be quiet, be quiet. You are not lost. You are not lost!" I paused. "We are only a few minutes away from the convoy. Pull yourself together! Pull yourself together in front of these soldiers. Think of your driver. Get it together. Take a breath."

She agreed and expressed gratitude as she overcame her fear.

Waiting a few seconds, I explained, "Everyone on our radio frequency heard your screams for help, and even worse, you read a grid coordinate over the radio. That was dangerous."

That statement got her attention.

She sheepishly stated, "Yes, I know. I am sorry, but I couldn't see anything. I don't know what happened, I got lost—"

Interrupting, "We can't discuss that now. The rest of DISCOM is expecting us back. If you are okay, let's get out of here."

She said she was okay.

Directing my driver to move sufficiently forward to form a march unit, we led the vehicles to rejoin the convoy.

I radioed my battalion commander that the captain and vehicles were back with the march unit.

I received, "Roger, over," from my battalion commander.

To that I responded, "Roger, out."

The convoy moved forward overnight into Iraq. We stopped in fishbone configuration; vehicles parked off both sides of the roadway, catercorner to each other with three or four vehicle links between each other. We waited for our next movement order. Exhausted, only a few people were milling about outside of their vehicles.

The spectacular view featured craters that were several stories deep and burned-out vehicles littering the landscape for miles. Everyone was mindful that we had crossed the line of departure and were in enemy territory.

CHAPTER 12

FAREWELL

———

In early afternoon Lieutenant Hemsley called me, "Ma'am, are you monitoring the radio? I was monitoring the radio, and I heard … I heard there has been an accident, and some of our guys were in it. Over."

I responded, "Roger, LT. I don't hear any activity on my radio frequency. Move to my location. Over."

"Moving Ma'am, Roger. Out."

While waiting for Hemsley, I alerted the first sergeant of a possible problem. He was certain all soldiers were on site except our track crews which were under battalion control and our contact teams deployed forward in support of division cavalry and combat service units.

When Hemsley arrived, radio traffic on the battalion frequency was confirming an accident.

Hemsley started talking, "Ma'am, something has happened to the guys on our tracks. Someone reported an incident to higher headquarters." He pointed, "An accident just happened over there where that smoke is coming up."

In the distance over my right shoulder a puff of smoke was floating in the air. I radioed battalion to let the commander know I was moving to check on my soldiers at the accident site.

My adrenaline was increasing; I was anxious, but I kept my bearing and my mind clear. My driver and I sped on and off the engineered trail taking the most direct route to the smoke.

The senior noncommissioned officer on site, Master Sergeant Mathews, walked to meet me when I arrived. I asked what happened and if everyone was okay.

He was solemn, "Yes Ma'am, Sergeant Fairhill and Private Hicks are dead."

My insides were screaming, *No, no, no, not dead!*

But I said, "Dead? Where are they?"

Walking beside Master Sergeant Mathews I was stoic and asked each person if he was okay.

The master sergeant stopped and motioned toward two ponchos lying on the ground, "They are over here, Ma'am."

Approaching disheveled legs extending from a poncho I asked, "What happened? I want to see them."

The master sergeant replied adamantly, "You don't want to see them Ma'am … you don't."

But I do; I want to see their faces. Reaching for a poncho Master Sergeant Mathews stretched his arm, "Please, Ma'am, don't do it. Don't! You don't want to see."

The intensity of his voice stopped me; I stood up.

Looking down at the ponchos, I asked again, "What happened, Sergeant Mathews?"

Looking at the ground he explained, "After entering Iraq through the lanes engineered for tracked vehicles we stopped here to assemble and wait for next instructions. Everyone was relaxed in or on their vehicles. I don't know why but Sergeant Fairhill and Private Hicks got off their vehicle. Some of the guys saw them looking at something and overheard one of them say, 'Hey, what is this?'

"I heard a loud Boom! A bomblet exploded. I ran over, but they were dead when I got there. I told the other soldiers to stay back—to remain where they were with their vehicles. I removed the ponchos off the bodies and covered them. Ma'am, I am so sorry."

Shaking my head in agreement, "I know Sergeant Mathews; I am sorry too."

As Master Sergeant Mathews spoke, my eyes were drawn to indications of the ferocity of the explosion and the frailty of human flesh.

We stood there for a while then walked away. I remember thinking, *There may be more bomblets, we need to get the other soldiers out of that location.* I lost track of time, but it seemed within fifteen minutes an ambulance team arrived to recover the bodies. Watching the doors close reminded me of my dad's funeral procession less than four months ago. I followed the ambulance as it moved slowly back to our battalion area.

My driver and I stopped at my company area as the ambulance continued to the quartermaster company that included graves registration in its mission.

My soldiers were quietly, respectfully moving about as the rumor of the soldiers' deaths spread. The first sergeant gathered the soldiers in one location where I officially announced our losses and gave everyone the opportunity to speak.

Within the hour I was relieved to hear our track crews had returned to the company so that those soldiers could get support from their friends and sergeants. The next day the battalion chaplain would visit. We just needed to get through tonight.

The sun fell behind the flat endless horizon, and darkness covered us like a thick black blanket. Alone in my vehicle, I tried to process the deaths of my soldiers. I didn't want to believe they were dead even though the sight of their covered bodies was fresh in my mind.

Thump, thump, thump …

I heard knocking on my vehicle door, "Ma'am, may I stay with you? I need more space." It was Lieutenant Cooper.

I responded, "Sure, lieutenant, you can stay."

He crawled in a back seat of my Humvee and started talking about the death of his soldiers. I shared everything I knew with him believing he had a right to know. We discussed what happened after the tracks left the company, but he was curious to know details I couldn't answer because I didn't know. I explained the Army would investigate, and that would be it. Adding, "We need to focus on our responsibilities and help our soldiers through our loss."

The evening passed as we talked about our dead … we both remembered that Sergeant Fairhill was first to volunteer to have me cut his hair with the company barber clippers.

We laughed, "I really did a pitiful job, didn't I? It was a mess, but he sat there like I was a professional barber."

Cooper said, "Yes, he was that kind of guy, Ma'am, always helpful and positive."

"Yes." I responded, "He was absolutely wonderful and a hard worker."

We had so many memories with him. He was young but had advanced fast in the Army. I was starting to relax as we shared many different memories …

"Click … Hummmm."

The sound sent chills over my body because I knew the mortuary unit had turned on its refrigeration unit, and their bodies were in there. I was touched by it. Lieutenant Cooper must have known what it meant, also, because he stopped talking. For a few moments we sat silently surrounded by the blackness of night.

After a few hours Lieutenant Cooper was asleep sitting up in one of the two back seats. He looks barely more than a child himself, but he was a leader. Very high energy and positive, prior service and tonight he showed me he cares about his soldiers. I admired that.

I remembered the company support meeting I held in the company recreation room before we left Fort Hood. Families from across the country seized the opportunity to say good-bye to their loved ones before they departed to war. The faces of the mothers, fathers, spouses, children, siblings, fiancés, and girlfriends sitting with my soldiers and listening to my address were fresh in my mind. I said, "I will do everything in my power to bring your loved ones back to you. Everything that I do will be directed to ensure our safe return."

The younger soldier, Private Hicks, arrived in the unit just before pack out and deployment. He graduated from high school last spring; the thought of that alone made me sad. Mourning Hicks and Sergeant Fairhill lay gently on top of the grief I felt for my father. I prayed for the families of my soldiers and my own family. As I sat quietly, again, my thoughts were drawn the sound of distant humming.

By nightfall the following day, Kuwait was free, and the war was declared over. Chaplains of various denominations visited my soldiers to provide individual or group grief counseling. I requested a memorial service for the unit. So, a few days later on a sunny day, two pairs of boots, two helmets, and dog tags for each soldier were displayed in front of a makeshift altar in honor of our fallen brothers. My soldiers were seated in a semicircle behind chairs reserved for our important guest; the battalion commander, DISCOM commander, and the assistant division command support (a one-star general). I really appreciated them coming to acknowledge the importance of the lives of my soldiers.

Before the memorial service started, the DISCOM commander spoke with me alone. He expressed sympathy and asked about my soldiers and the unit as a whole. Our conversation was pleasant until he asked, "What race were they, the soldiers who were killed?" I didn't know why he asked me that.

I told him, "Thank you Sir for your concern, everyone is doing alright …" Taking a shallow breath I answered his other question, "They both were White Sir, the soldiers killed were White."

I waited for his reaction because his question implied race makes a difference. He stated emotionlessly, "I am sorry to hear they were killed."

Nodding I responded, "Thank you Sir, I am sorry, too."

A lot of things had crossed my mind after the soldier's tragedy, but skin color wasn't one of them. What difference could that make? We were all Americans, and we were all human beings.

Race seemed to be the driving force and the Achilles heel for this man. He didn't mind showing me his personal racial insensitivity that appeared to narrow his perspective and understanding making him seem blunt and unempathetic.

Who knows what made him ask me the race of the soldiers? He could have found that information from a variety of sources before seeing me. I considered him a White supremacist; therefore, the death of a White person would be a greater loss than that of a person who was not White. I can barely stand to be around him, my battalion commander, and his motley crew of followers. The commanders have made it clear to me that they care more about race than performance. I didn't trust them, but I had to work with them, so I tolerated them like I would gnats swarming around to annoy me.

The memorial service was short and respectful and featured prayer, reflections, a eulogy, rollcall, and a bugler who played a ceremony farewell called "Taps." As a company we really missed our guys, but we didn't obsess over our grief. When it was over; our guests talked in a group before the general left the area.

The noncommissioned officers held formation to ensure everyone was okay.

After that day no one spoke to me about our dead, but I knew they were missed. The officer investigating the incident did not interview me, and I did not get to read his final report.

Within days our division moved back into Saudi Arabia. My prayers were answered; and there was peace.

CHAPTER 13

ABOVE THE EARTH

———

"Ka-boom … boom … boom!"

One night, I was awakened—startled by the sound of thunder rolling in the distance and the rustling sound of my canvas tent tossing about in the wind. The weather was changing. Increasingly warm temperatures caused thunderstorms. An early spring storm was coming to the desert of Saudi Arabia. As it moved closer, I felt vibrations from the lightening striking the flat desert through my cot.

The tent stakes that held the bottom of my tent to the ground were pulled loose by the force of the wind allowing me to see shades of light.

As the wind intensified, I believed the tent was going to blow away. The storm was fierce unlike anything I had experienced. I wondered how my soldiers in their tents larger than mine were doing. I listened to hear voices, but all I heard was the crackling sounds of lightning as it streaked across the sky and the over-lapping sounds of booming thunder.

My heart was beating hard and fast as if I were running a marathon. I slipped myself deep into my sleeping bag, closed my eyes, and prayed.

I believe I was wide awake trying to turn over, but I was petrified, so I controlled my breathing to avoid panicking.

I couldn't explain what happened next, but, suddenly, I was in a different place, standing on firm ground. The storm had passed because I couldn't hear anything nor could I see anything through dense, thick clouds, much like in a steam room.

I could sense the presence of people near me. I found comfort in the thought that perhaps my soldiers were with me.

In the distance, I knew intuitively that an enemy force was advancing to engage us by foot. I heard them marching, approaching us in formation.

Sounds of clanging and ringing as metal hitting metal started and got increasingly louder as they surrounded me. My forces were fully engaged in battle and fighting hard because I heard the moans and groans of the injured and the thud of dead falling.

I felt the enemy getting close to me; I didn't want him to strike me first. Struggling, I touched my weapon which allowed me to see myself … dressed in armor like a Roman Centurion with a breast plate, knickerbockers skirt, helmet, knee high boots, a sword, and shield.

I was tense, fearlessly anticipating contact with the enemy, wanting to strike him, but the cloud that was blocking my visibility now reflected the glinting shine off my armor.

My right hand was on my sword as I readied to strike my adversaries. I steadied my grip. Triggered by the force of a warm breath on my neck, I swung into the cloud with all my strength.

I hit something, so I continued to swing, strike, and duck to defend my ground. With each strike, my enemy was hit. I could feel my blade cutting through its flesh, and I heard cries for help as the swing of my blade was cutting the air. I continued to swing as hard as I could, grunting with every motion! The fight was ferocious. I gave it all I had, I was a warrior, fighting with the strength of an Army.

I felt the heaviness of the shield, the tight fit of my helmet, and the tremendous weight of my sword, but I was neither tired, nor sweaty.

Then I heard music and sounds of distant thunder that said, "***Who is the king of glory? The Lord strong and mighty in battle. Lift up your head, that the king of glory may come in.***" (Psalms 24:8–10, New International Version)

The battle was over, but I held my stance as the cloud slowly lifted uncovering a quiet battlefield. I was standing on a hill overlooking thousands of slain enemy bodies littering the rolling hills below, covering the terrain for miles in every direction. I didn't recognize any of them. They were not my soldiers, not of my kind. No one and nothing was moving. I was alone. The tip of my sword, held in my right hand, was planted in the soil. My feet were spread apart, pressed into the dirt, and a red robe that looks like a cape was blowing in the breeze in tandem with my full head of Afro hair.

My face was tight; teeth were clenched. My helmet was in my left hand, placed over my heart.

I didn't move as the sun broke through revealing soft clouds and a blue sky. I stood in victory, resilient and strong in the Word of God filled with the Holy Spirit forged into a new life … and a new creation.

Within a flash, I was transitioned back to my tent where I stood next to my cot looking at my body lying in my sleeping bag … then I felt myself rising higher and higher at an accelerated, speed racing through the universe high above the earth. My peripheral vision caught shades of color like layers of a rainbow. It was so beautiful; it filled me with happiness and joy. I can't describe the adulation I felt. The heavens were endless, with areas of both darkness and light, and bright in many colors and hues. A light glowing through thick fluffy white clouds was far in the distance. It was perfect. Touches of blue, orange, pink, and red lit the background like at sunrise. This place was awesome, and I felt at one with it. I looked down to see myself but found that I was too small to be seen; those things considered big on earth were smaller than specks of dirt, so insignificant that I could only feel their existence. From there, what was large on earth was nothing. Looking across what seemed infinite, I had peace. I felt it like I never had before and held on to it … I wanted to stay in that space.

My eyes opened. Blinking into consciousness, I realized I was still in my tent in Saudi Arabia. Slowly looking around my tent, I wept. I was overwhelmed but memory of what I just experienced. So beautiful and so peaceful.

Seated on the edge of my cot, I questioned my place in military service for the first time. Why was I here? There seemed to be no logical reason for me to stay in the Army— no reason to battle the hatred, injustice, discrimination that dominated the system. Like in my dreams, I believe it was time for me to transition from a warrior to a woman of peace.

I had fought my final battle.

"Company!" Looking at my watch, I saw it was late. The first sergeant was holding morning formation; I needed to get out of here.

"Platoon!" The platoon sergeants echo.

"Attention!" The first sergeant said with power.

I rush to clean up and dress; I put on my cap and stand strong as I walk out of my tent.

CHAPTER 14

LEAKING VESSEL

——

I left part of myself in the desert. The callousness of my leaders, the death of my father, and the blood of my soldiers required renewal of my spirit and steadfastness of my faith. I didn't let anyone know, but when alone I wept like a leaking vessel full of water.

We received our redeployment sequence and were awaiting our flight manifest. Living quarters were greatly improved after we were relocated to some Saudi apartment buildings. Our equipment was at sea, sailing back home. Now, I had time to meet with some of the Black officers I had not seen in a while. Thank God, we all survived; we experienced many incidences of abuse and mistreatment, but we survived.

Seeing friends and being in a safe space where I could be myself was good. After usual hugs and greetings, we started laughing and talking about the look on the faces in the crowd as I briefed the DISCOM commander and his guest in his briefing tent a few months prior.

Marilynn said, "From where I sat in the back all I could see was neck because they were holding their heads down. Cleo, you took them to school."

I stated, "They were stunned beyond words; at least I didn't hear a word. The DISCOM commander turned in his seat to ask for questions, but I didn't hear any, did you Marilynn?"

"No, Ma'am, not a word. I don't think some of them knew what you were saying."

"Marilynn, I don't know what they wanted to accomplish and why McAfee chose customer service as the topic."

Marilynn joined in. "They greatly underestimated you, my friend. It was a night to remember. Valerie, our girl made me proud."

"I wonder why you weren't invited, Valerie." I paused.

"Cleola, until we talked days later, I didn't know you were in my company area."

We were pretending to be back to normal, be we had been abused. I began to talk openly about my experiences especially about the loss of my soldiers. Marilynn and Valerie listened quietly.

Valerie, the DISCOM headquarters and headquarters company commander, shared some of her experiences that were very much akin to mine. Officers on the DISCOM commander staff—which included the Materiel Management Center—were rude and disrespectful to her because they could be rude without fear of punitive recourse. She told us how the staff complained about something different every day. One officer complained about something wrong with his vehicle everyday as if she was a mechanic. He harassed her.

I noticed Valerie sounded upbeat when describing her abuse. I did it too when laughing at the attendees of that briefing. We were pushing through, but our situation wasn't funny; it was discrimination, abuse, and much more. I will not laugh at it again.

After an hour, we departed with our usual hugs and words of encouragement, then departed to our quarters in distant locations. Farewell my friends, until I see you at Fort Hood.

Thank goodness the flight manifests for my unit had arrived, and we were going home.

I had done my job; my soldiers were on their way back home to their families. As the plane lifted off the desert, I closed my eyes; the sight of my fallen soldier's bodies revisited me. They were not forgotten; why should I forget them? They were now eternally part of United States military history and perhaps my history. I opened my Bible and read until I fell asleep.

Hours later the plane landed at Grey Airfield near Fort Hood. Buses were visibly lined up bumper-to-bumper, ready to carry us to our drop off point at the gym. Spirits were upbeat as we passed familiar sights on Fort Hood. The soldiers clapped and cheered when passing landmarks they missed like the post exchange, commissary, and the bowling alley.

As we exited the buses, the noncommissioned officers called a battalion formation then turned the formation to the officers. My battalion commander led his battalion into the gym where families and friends were cheering with balloons and flowers in the bleachers under bright glaring lights. I marched in front of my company.

When the order was given, "Dismissed!" people ran out of the stands. The moment was joyous. The weight of 200 people lifted off my shoulders. I moved smiling and shaking hands, but inside I felt numb. Chief Warrant Officer (retired) Porter was the only face I recognized in the crowd. He smiled and greeted the troops. I made my way to the door and glanced back. I got them home and turned them over to their families; I whispered, "Thank God."

Before we took leave, the first sergeant made certain the barracks and offices were operational. After leave ended our equipment returned and our shop operations started to build in tempo until it was completely operational.

I was told the parents of one of my deceased soldiers were on their way to Fort Hood. I reported their potential arrival to battalion, thinking the commander or maybe the division public affairs officer or an assigned escort officer would receive them and speak with them.

But, two days later, the parents of the younger deceased soldier Private Hicks entered the Orderly Room door. I didn't know protocols, but they were at Fort Hood, and they were welcome, like family.

I introduced myself and offered them a seat in my office before closing the door for privacy.

The soldier's mother asked if I was surprised to see them. I admitted that I was surprised.

After a few minutes she patted tears from her face.

Walking across to her I asked if we could hug. She nodded yes and we hugged. What a bittersweet moment; I needed that hug, too.

I said "I am so sorry, Ma'am. Your son was a great man, and a wonderful soldier."

After a while I returned to my desk. I could see they were consumed with grief. They had driven from a northern Midwestern state to meet the soldiers who knew their son. They wanted to know details of what happened to him. So, I told them every fact I knew.

His mother admitted to hoping for a miracle, that there had been a mistake and that her son had returned with the company. I asked if they had a funeral for him. They had a funeral, but the body was not viewable, so they did not see the body.

Hick's father shared his fantasy: his son was on a secret operation that required him to disappear for a while; that would explain why they had not heard from him. I explained I saw their son and he was dead. I was deeply sorry.

His mother said their military escort told them two people were killed; one of them picked up a bomblet. They wanted to know which soldier picked it up.

I told her the truth; I wasn't aware if anyone knew the answer to that question. But I assured her neither of them would deliberately cause harm to the other. I shared the company grieved the loss of her son. We talked for a while. If there was anything I could do for them, I would.

They were easy to talk with—truly beautiful people longing for their son. They wanted to meet the soldiers closest to him. The first sergeant set up the visit and Lieutenant Cooper was their escort.

Before they left my office, I hugged them both. When separating, his mother pulled a small professional photograph of Hicks out her pocket and placed it in my hand. I thanked her and promised to never forget him. And I did not.

Then Lieutenant Cooper arrived and took care of them. My heart was so broken for those parents. I hope our visit brought them some comfort.

Within days we were preparing for the battalion change of command. Yep, the man who had done so much to drive me out of command had come to the end of his time in the battalion.

The new battalion commander was allegedly a general's son. To me that means he was on the fast track to become a general officer. That was how it went. Ingrained in officer culture is the ridiculous supposition that leadership positions should be passed thought bloodlines, gender, educational institute, and finally but least, natural talent and hard work.

The new battalion commander was eager to get the battalion to a high state of readiness. I liked his energy. During my initial office call with the commander, tears streamed uncontrollably down my cheeks. This was the first time I had cried publicly; embarrassed, I apologized as I wiped my face. I guess I was suffering the effects of trauma inflected by my time deployed.

The new commander was trying to motivate his unit, but we were done. Despite my exhaustion and emptiness, I gave my all to exceed requirements.

The battalion commander started a friendly competition for best company. My company won the first two months. Before announcing the third month's winner, the commander explained to me in a private meeting, "Cleola, I am changing the competition criteria to let another unit win. You have the numbers, but I want the competition to motivate everybody to do their best. Right now, it is starting to look like your company is unbeatable … which defeats my purpose. So, I can't let your company win this month."

He was smiling and so was I because I did not care.

I understood what he was saying and what he was doing, but did I think it was right? No! It wasn't right.

He wanted another unit to win … so he changed the rules so the unit that earned the win would lose, and a lesser unit would win without earning it … because the win would make the lesser unit feel good and it would serve his purpose. He forgot about the broken spirit of the unit that rightfully won. He would break their morale and frustrate their efforts.

Wow, he doesn't see dishonesty in what he is doing? He is lying, cheating and lowering standards at the same time! The Army has manufactured another 'leader.'

Smiling at him, I shook my head. Thinking … *I am ready to get away from him!*

This was the perfect metaphor for why abuse and racial discrimination thrived in the Army, and why my past battalion commander believed it alright to torture me for two years. His hate wasn't personal; he just wanted someone other than me to command my company during combat. So, he set up false premises and conditions for me to fail, so he could justify my relief and replace me with someone he wanted.

I only had a few weeks left in command. My successor would begin his thirty-day change of command inventory in less than two weeks, and we would change command a few days after the inventory was complete.

My company command ended very much as it began, on a beautiful sunny day in September exactly twenty-four months from the day it started. My mother was there. The company was accounted for and ready to be passed on. I was emotional about leaving, but I couldn't let it show. My band of brothers and sisters who would never leave my heart stood in front of me in formation. The soldiers, alive and dead, that made up this great company—forever, I salute them.

The first sergeant called, "Company!"

Platoon sergeants responded, "Platoon."

The first sergeant ordered, "Attention!"

The soldiers responded. "Raise up maintenance!"

CHAPTER 15

WE ALL WANTED TO GO

I dragged the weight of the years of bullying and abuse received at Fort Hood with me to the officer's staff course, Combined Arms Services and Staff School, at Fort Leavenworth, Kansas. My sensitivities to racism and discrimination were at their peak because I experienced it daily during my command. After what I experienced, I believe military culture was deliberately structured to oppress some and to feed the racist appetites of others.

In my seat I looked around the classroom that was structured to psychologically create a space of White male dominance and perpetual spaces of isolation and subjugation for people like me. I was the only Black female in the class; there was one White female, one Black male, and the remainder in a class of ten to twelve were White males. That was the normal way the Army diversified. The classrooms I've seen have always been similarly structured. I believe this climate gave people like Major McAfee and my past battalion commander and the DISCOM commander a false sense of self-worth, entitlement, and an unrealistic sense of power over others. Like I said in "Like Wild Dogs," their strength lay in their numbers, and in the Army, they were always the majority.

The officer instructor started the class making comments about people who went to the war that lasted a few hours. I laughed along with him because this was a pass or fail course, that I took to fulfilling an Army requirement. I planned to relax and unwind here. The only thing important to me was the scheduled visit from the Logistics Assignments Branch and Officers Records. My command predecessor was still in that job, so I expected to see him.

About midcourse, the logistics assignment general and his staff arrived from Department of the Army in Washington, DC to discuss future assignments, current policies, and career paths. As scheduled, the logistics officers gathered in a classroom to hear General Martin, the logistics chief of personnel management.

We were at attention as he entered, "Take your seats … take your seats." The general was cordial, full of one-liner jokes that caused laughter. I listened but my only interest was the location of my next assignment.

At the end of his talk, before we were released to meet individually with our assignment officer, the general said casually, "One more thing, for all who have asked, the deployment to Desert Shield/Desert Storm will not count; people who went will not have a career advantage over those who did not go. We've received so many inquiries, questions, and concerns that we have decided that it will not count."

Now, my attention was piqued. After all my battalion commander put me through, worried about me as a 'future general,' the leadership in Washington, DC had devised a resolution for his concerns—changing the rules. This was a moment where a cursing woman would cuss! I didn't know anything about the 'future general' rule until my battalion commander brought it up. I believed it was his paranoid obsession until the moment the general said there were inquires, questions, and concerns ... do you mean a rule really existed?

I didn't say anything until the general asked for questions, "Sir, did you say deployment to Iraq for Desert Shield/Desert Storm will not count for the officers who deployed?"

The general responded, "Yes, the officers who went will not be favored over the officers who did not go." He spoke as if that was the answer I wanted to hear.

I asked, "Why doesn't it count, Sir?"

His facial expression changed to that of curiosity.

My voice was strong; I was sure he heard me, "We are the best trained soldiers in the Army. More to the point Sir, we are better than trained. The officers who didn't go are trained; we are combat veterans—veterans of a foreign war. We are experienced and our knowledge has been tested; that can't be denied. We lived in the dirt month after month, wearing Kevlar, flight vests, and boots 24/7, without bathing and bathrooms, living in tents with dirt flooring, on a cot, away from family, missing holidays, the birth of children, away from new born babies, small children, and dying parents."

Silence hung in the air for a few seconds, but it seemed like a long time before the general answered, "We have given this a lot of thought. I want you to know that there was a lot of discussion and considerations given to all sides."

He didn't have any trouble sharing the credit for the decision once I raised a question. Stating "We have given it a lot of thought." Well, just because there was more than one decisionmaker doesn't mean their decision wasn't conceived in malice.

I continued, "Sir, it counted for our other branches and even other service branches like the Marines—for everyone except Army logisticians? Our work in support of the battle—in support of those units—doesn't count? President Bush led an estimated 800,000 people in a star-spangled salute to Desert Storm warriors, the biggest victory celebration since the end of World War II. Crowds roared as Gen. Norman Schwarzkopf brought 8,800 of his troops, some marching and others riding in armored vehicles, on a 2.5-mile parade down Constitution Avenue, past the White House and across the Memorial Bridge. They were celebrated for their service. As you know, Sir, logisticians were included in that parade as were warriors, part of the fighting force that was victorious in battle and celebrated by the American public." (Ferraro, 1991)

Standing in front of his chair, the general looked at the floor as if thinking of a response. I believe he was searching for a way to explain why senior logistics officers, flag officers, and agencies had decided to minimize our combat service while the president of the United States was publicly celebrating us as warriors and heroes. They had no respect for neither soldiers like me nor the American citizens, deceiving them with their fake salute to the troops. I felt like little more than a political pawn. Now I didn't respect them, either.

He responded, "You are right … you are right; you have worked hard, and the country thanks you for your service, but it doesn't count because other people wanted to go and didn't get the opportunity; we all wanted to go."

I could have fallen over. That was an honest answer if I've ever heard one. They wanted to go but couldn't go so my going doesn't count. I believed him.

Outwardly this general didn't look like much. He appeared gaunt and a little older than most officers of his rank, but with others his influence cast a long shadow over structures of diversity and justice when maintaining leadership in the Army; therefore, what he said that day would stand absolute and unchallenged.

He looked uncomfortable. I thought he knew his answer to my question sounded ridiculous, and he probably didn't mean to tell the truth, but he did, and I appreciated it.

I thought of my fallen soldiers, "Sir, may I ask one more thing?"

He nodded, "Yes."

"What about the people who lost their lives? Do they count? How can they not count? Some people died; will they be denied their rightful place with those who have died in other wars?"

He answered, but I didn't care to listen. Of course, he counted the dead, it is the living they are not counting. I stood until he stopped talking, then sat down, smiling. Why should I continue to question him? He had answered my question; "they all wanted to go."

I remembered something my first DISCOM commander in Korea told me during my initial meeting with him, "Davis you can be the best and know it, but if they say you are not the best, you are not." I didn't understand him then, but now I do.

I doodled while others asked more questions. I neither cared about that general nor the wolves he represented. He was nothing to me but a man in a uniform. I waited to get my next assignment, which I hoped would be Korea.

"Group, Attention!"

Oh, has he finished? I stood to attention. *Where is the door?* I walked past the general carefully avoiding visual contact and holding my breath so he and I couldn't breathe the same air.

THE LORD, MIGHTY IN BATTLE

In my room after dinner, I fought back tears that swelled every time I remembered my dream experience fighting in the clouds. Since then, I felt differently. I was dealing with something I could not define. That night, I decided to share the overwhelming sensations I experienced with a friend who was a chaplain. He was quiet as I expressed my feelings as best I could. The memory of every detail caused me to traverse emotions between exuberance and tears. When I finished, he didn't have questions. He simply said, "Cleola do you have your Bible, New International Version nearby? First read these two verses; if you have questions after reading them, call me back."

I relaxed at my desk; I read … (Ephesians 6:10–17)

"…be strong in the Lord and in his mighty power. Put on the full armor of God, so that you can take your stand against the devil's schemes. For our struggle is not against flesh and blood, but against the rulers, against the author-ities, against the powers of this dark world, and against the spiritual forces of evil in the heavenly realms. Therefore, put on the full armor of God, so that when the day of evil comes, you may be able to stand your ground, and after you have done everything, to stand. Stand firm then, with the belt of truth buckled around your waist, with the breastplate of righteousness in place, and with your feet fitted with the readiness that comes from the gospel of peace. In addition to all this, take up the shield of faith, with which you can extinguish all the flaming arrows of the evil one. Take the helmet of salvation and the sword of the Spirit, which is the word of God."

I flipped to (Psalm 24) as tears streamed down my face, *"Who may ascend the mountain of the Lord? Who may stand in his holy place? The one who has clean hands and a pure heart, who does not trust in an idol or swear by a false god. They will receive blessing from the Lord and vindication from God their Savior. Such is the generation of those who seek him, who seek your face, God … Lift up your heads, you gates; be lifted up, you ancient doors, that the King of glory may come in. Who is this King of glory? The Lord strong and mighty, the Lord mighty in battle. Lift up your heads, you gates; lift them up, you ancient doors, that the King of glory may come in. Who is he, this King of glory? The Lord Almighty— he is the King of glory."*

When I finished, I sobbed as I read the verses repeatedly, recognizing the similarities between my dream and these scriptures. I said aloud, "Who is the King of glory, the Lord mighty in battle." I heard these words in the dream.

The Lord had fought my battle. I felt differently about the Army because I was done with the Army.

I stood to get a tissue from a box. As I stretched out my right hand; I remembered the briefing in the desert: my stance at modified "at ease," the tip of my pointer now touching the ground, both arms along my sides. My breaths were shallow, the people—some I didn't know—seated in the tent. I walked out undefeated. Everything I needed was provided, and I was not defeated.

After a good cry I was okay; I am humbled.

I didn't have any questions for the chaplain, and I didn't have any more tears to shed. I was changed. I looked forward to a space where I could mourn my dad, heal from the abusive command environment, and find peace.

CHAPTER 16

SHE'S IN CHARGE

———

Bingo! I made it back to Korea, and the best thing happened; my supervisor and the installation commander, Colonel Younger, was a woman. I was so happy. No matter what, she couldn't be worse than the horrible demons I'd served with in other assignments.

I had a great job now, too—director of logistics for the installation, which was the senior logistics position on the commander's staff. A position ranked for a lieutenant colonel. And I was so happy to be back in a culture that was polite, safe, and had delicious food. The local Korean bulgogi houses had the best seasoned meats and seafood served on rice, with kimchi, lettuce, and garlic. Thinking of it made my mouth water.

Lush green rice paddy fields surround our installation located in the middle of South Korea near the city of Pyeongtaek which was about a one-hour bus ride from the big city of Seoul.

So how did I get so lucky, to hold a key staff position on a beautiful small military post led by a woman? Well, the process took about four months from when I arrived in Korea.

At my initial in-processing, I thought I was going back to a unit in division, a place that was like home to me in the northern part of the country. I held many wonderful memories of my first assignment at Camp Casey: my loving church family, the grace and power of the DISCOM Chapel choir, long fitness runs, and hard work. I had hoped to go back to the serenity of the mountains for spiritual renewal, mourning, and healing.

But upon arrival my orders assigned me to the Theater Support Command Headquarters near the city of Taegu (now Daegu), in the southern part of the country.

Once there, I was greeted by my supervisor Colonel Richardson, the theater assistant chief of staff, logistics who had been waiting for me to arrive to replace a captain who was leaving to take command. At our first meeting Colonel Richardson seemed impressed with my officer evaluation brief. I watched as he quickly read my past assignments loud enough for me to hear: "Platoon leader and company executive officer in the Corp Support Command; battalion maintenance officer, shop officer, and materiel maintenance officer at division here in Korea; and maintenance officer on the division general's staff, battalion operations officer, and two years of company command during Desert Shield and Desert Storm at Fort Hood … and you are still a captain."

I answered, "Yes, sir."

He said something like, "I don't see many captain's records like this."

I smiled, nodded my head without engaging him in discussion about my record.

From the start, my relationship with my peers was okay. We worked in a large room, with a few cubicles but mostly open from desk to desk. Our work didn't overlap, so other than greetings we didn't say much to each other, and that was fine. Everyone was professional.

It was winter and cold when I arrived but soon the weather was warming, and Korea dressed itself in beautiful pink cherry blossoms, ornamental trees, and freshly planted green rice saplings.

One day in staff meeting Colonel Richardson announced he would host a section cookout at his quarters, on a Saturday afternoon; I was invited, so of course, I went.

Richardson said to dress in casual attire, so I wore a mint green and white short set, a pair of cloth shoes with a one-inch heel, and earrings.

The gathering was okay; the colonel and his wife were welcoming, and everyone was friendly. I interacted with everyone. This was a "small talk" affair, and I was very good at making small talk because I enjoyed the arts, which provided a plethora of topics to talk about. Purposely, I was not the first or second to leave. All things considered I enjoyed the event.

The following Monday, a note was on my desk from the colonel stating, "See Me." I rushed to his office. Richardson appeared annoyed when I entered his office. His face was scowled as if something was wrong; I immediately thought of my mother or family in the states. He told me to have a seat; my heart quickened, bracing for news from home. Richardson looked up from a paper on his desk, "Captain Davis, you are not a team player."

What? I was confused. I sat quietly.

"You are being counseled for not being a team player."

Did he say, counseled? OK, I will bite, "Sir, what did I do?" I looked at him, cheekbones high, eager to hear the excuse he was using to counsel me.

He continued, "When you came to the cookout at my house, you dressed up, and everyone else was wearing jeans, making yourself stick out different from everyone else."

I forced myself to hold my face still. This would be laughable if he had not said this was counseling. I would not accept counseling because my clothing was not to his liking.

I responded, "Sir, you said the attire was casual. To me, I dressed casually. I didn't wear jeans because I don't own a pair of jeans. But I would have bought a pair if you had said wear jeans."

I knew this is a cultural difference; I would never attend a party at a house in jeans. To me, it was the equivalent to wearing rags. According to the etiquette I was raised into, short pants are casual by definition. At home I would have worn a dress or slacks and a top to such an event.

Richardson added, "That isn't the only thing. You act like you are better than everyone else, the way you carry yourself."

Now, he had gone too far. The audacity of him to say that I thought I was better. I didn't, but so what if I did? And what did he mean by "the way I carry myself"?

"Colonel Richardson, I don't know what you mean."

"Captain Davis, you look down on people and intimidate people." He paused, "And there is an air of superiority about you that I don't like."

And for me that did it—"air of superiority"? From my perspective, this meeting had turned into a ditch. I was offended that he believed he could counsel me on the superior way I carry myself. I wondered what suggestions he had for me to fix my problem; be less superior? His accusations were unjust, unfounded, childish, and silly. His face looked red and his lips tight, posturing as if he was angry. Speaking of a communication gap, we were in two different worlds. I had no idea what he meant.

I spoke calmly, "Sir, I attended your cookout because you invited me, and I thought I was welcomed at your house, but your perception of my self-importance and my interpretation of casual dress has nothing to do with my work. I am respectful and kind to everyone I encounter. I didn't mean to offend you; please accept my apology for what I wore to your house. But, Sir, I can't let you counsel me because you don't like the clothes, or that you don't like the way I carry myself. I request to leave your office to seek an office call with Colonel Lindenberg."

Lindenberg, the theater chief of staff, was Richardson's rater and my senior rater.

Without another word I stood, saluted, and, respectfully leaving his office, I strolled down the hall to the get on the chief of staff's calendar.

When I explained what happened, Colonel Lindenberg was surprised to hear the content of my discussion with Richardson. Lindenberg said he had only heard that I was outstanding.

Colonel Lindenberg found me a new position. I was just passing through that place, hopefully headed to a better assignment to a space where I could have peace. Anyway, I was out of there! Happiness was the moment I saw Taegu in my rear-view mirror. Good-bye, Taegu!

So, there I was in beautiful Camp Humphreys in a great job working with wonderful people and working for Colonel Younger.

In my first staff meeting Colonel Younger introduced me and made her position clear, "Captain Davis is in the installation logistics office, and she has the full authority of the position, including the quarters authorized to the position in the command housing area, so I suggest you get to know her."

Wow, she supported me. That was great feeling.

She was the first woman of senior rank I had ever seen in charge, and she didn't take any mess. Since most of my career was in a division, the command climate was completely different. When those battalion commanders tried to challenge her or even talk down to her, she was boisterous and didn't hesitate to question them for questioning her. Boy, I loved it; she was in charge, and I was proud to stand by her side. I kept a natural smile on my face during that assignment.

She was strong and kind. She cared for everyone and led without prejudice. I needed to see her leadership style when I did. She was different but just as affective. That became one of my favorite assignments. At the end, I was thankful for the privilege to work with her. She gave me hope for the Army. I enjoyed my tour with her and sincerely wished her well.

CHAPTER 17

TRUE TO HIS WORD

This job started off messy. I held the position comparable to that of my supervisor's while at Fort Hood before I took my company command.

My new job position was the support operations officer, in the support squadron, at Fort Polk, Louisiana. My work position was under the responsibility of the Regimental Support Squadron Operations section. It sounds complicated but it's simple—a squadron is comparable to a battalion in a regiment; and think of a regiment as a robust independent brigade.

The squadron operations officer, Major Ladd, was my supervisor.

Less than a week on the job I had my newcomer's officer call with the regimental support squadron commander. I arrived with my cheekbones high. He stated my officer evaluation record was outstanding.

"Captain Davis, you obviously know a lot about logistics. Now this is what I want you to do."

I had my pen and notebook out, "Yes, Sir?"

"Your number one priority is to make Major Ladd successful."

This was new; my supervisor's success was my priority. What kind of crazy unprofessional command guidance was that? It sounded as if he had tied my success to hers? To me, his statement implied that I was not only her subordinate but subservient to my supervisor as well, and that would never be. Maybe he meant my priority was to make the regiment successful or to make my section successful, or since this was my in-briefing maybe he meant to tell me how he would make me successful. If doing my job to the best of my ability contributed to her success, great, but she would not be my priority. I would help her if asked, but I would not train her. It seemed the commander had no confidence in Major Ladd's abilities.

I continued to listen to the squadron commander, completed my visit with him, and left.

I remembered self-training on the job, to learn the responsibilities of the battalion operations officer. The nights I stayed up reading Army field manuals working under the pressure of the forthcoming evaluation at the National Training Center. My battalion commander showed little interest in my professional development; instead, he made jokes with my fellow members. But I learned the job through trial and error; I pushed myself so hard to learn everything I could about operations and tactics.

The longer I stayed in the Army the more I saw how the other system worked. I believe Major Ladd was "somebody's girl"; therefore, she would be promoted if she kept her nose clean. But right now, the commander needed someone to do her job, so he told me to do it. Maybe if I made her successful, her mentor would help me, too. I could become a "good ole girl," sliding from job to job letting someone do my work. But no, that way was not for me; I was a professional officer, professional logistician, and a professional leader.

The squadron commander's intuition was correct; Major Ladd needed a lot of help, but she was not going to get it from me because she was a poor leader who thought yelling within inches of my face was an effective way to motivate me. I regularly found myself in her office as she yelled at me because she had missed something. It seemed she didn't know how to ask for help. Sometimes I would direct her to the appropriate regulation. I wondered how she became a field-grade officer without knowing what an operations officer did.

One day she said, "You intimidate me, Captain Davis, and make me feel inept." I really dislike comments like that. I didn't make her feel inept; she felt that way because she was inept. I didn't do anything to intimidate her either; those field manuals she wouldn't read were what intimidated her.

During our first field exercise, things didn't operate very well. Instead of asking for help, she walked up within an inch of my face, scolding me in front of my troops and everyone in our work area because her operations order lacked details sufficient to synchronize operations with the regiment. This time I didn't take her scolding quietly. I showed her the logistics support plan which was completed and in execution. I pointed to the truckmaster, a sergeant first class who was standing within a few feet. I explained I was there to report the status of the missions that took place that morning and to adjust plans for future missions. The companies were briefed and were executing tasks to support the tactical squadrons as planned. She started to back away. I didn't have anything to do with what was going wrong because it fell under operations.

I said, "Major Ladd, everything that I didn't do is your job." Until that day, I don't think she understood the difference between her responsibilities in operations and mine in support operations. Now the differences were made clear.

Within a few months Christmas was coming, and I was tasked to plan and host a day-long regimental Christmas event that included multiple meals and multiple entertainment events for all ages. The regimental commander put his touch on it; he personally gave me guidance, so I knew it was important to him. At the end of our office call, he asked if I had questions, and I said, "Yes, Sir. The regiment doesn't have a job that will advance my career. I am overqualified for the position I presently hold. I would like your help in getting a job I have not done and that would advance my career."

He said, "Do a good job on this Christmas Party."

I responded, "Yes, Sir," and smiled.

The party was phenomenal. The regimental commander was very satisfied. True to his word, I was moved to the regimental combat support squadron. The combat support squadron was not structurally authorized. The companies were authorized but the command structure was not. It was created to consolidate operational control of the separate combat support companies: engineer, signal, air defense artillery, and chemical. The squadron was being deactivated. I would be the squadron executive officer through the deactivation ceremony which was within fewer than ninety days. I jumped at the opportunity to leave support squadron.

My new squadron commander and I worked well together. I worked hard to support him and to take care of the staff and his company commanders. I wanted to prove to myself that I could be a good executive officer.

The job was big, and I enjoyed my work environment. Within my second week on the job, the chemical company commander reported a lieutenant missing. Missing as in, she could not be found. The squadron personnel officer asked for advice before sending personnel stats to Regimental

Headquarters. Immediately, a squadron searched for her and notified military police. The lieutenant was last seen the first day of their field training exercise. She was not in her quarters at Bachelor Officer Quarters.

Her car was parked in our squadron parking area. The squadron commander was very concerned for her safety and so was I. I knew the lieutenant from her position in the support squadron; her disappearance was out of character for her. Also, I was personally involved because I was child sitting her nine-year-old niece while she was in the field. The exercise was to last four days.

Days passed without contact from the lieutenant. While the unit was packing to return from the field, she was discovered in good health, in the back of an ambulance. She had been there all along. Her soldiers brought her food and hid her. She asked them to keep her location secret and they did. Her behavior was strange, so when she got to Squadron Headquarters, I escorted her to the hospital where she was kept for about a week, then released her back to work. Her company commander was glad to have her back and so was I.

On the day scheduled, the lieutenant didn't pick up her niece. She didn't contact me, and I couldn't contact her, so I kept the child one more night. Saturday evening, we agreed to meet at a restaurant. Her niece was with me. The lieutenant looked okay, but something was different. She had a dazed look in her eyes. She was sighing. As we talked, she accused her niece of trying to harm her, stating the child had done this to her before and that she was afraid of her niece. The little girl was sitting across from her, listening. This sounded crazy, but I didn't know their history. *What is going on?* Instinctively, I wanted to protect the child. I asked if I should keep her niece a while longer, until arrangements could be made to send the child home. The lieutenant agreed to make arrangements. We finished our meal and went our separate ways.

On Monday morning, the lieutenant was absent from duty. Her car was gone from her quarters, and she had not been seen by any of her neighbors. The process started over again; I contacted the police. I disclosed everything I knew to both the squadron commander and the military police. Days passed without hearing from the lieutenant, then she started calling me at my home late at night, numerous times a night. Sometimes she didn't say anything, just grunts and sighs. She was ill, and I was afraid for her. I begged her to return to post to get help.

Because I had the lieutenant's niece, I developed a routine to give me time to drop her off at youth camp before fitness training started at 0600 hours. I worked every minute of the day, picked up the child, prepared our meals, and prepared for the next day. I had become a full-time single mom. She was a beautiful, smart, well-mannered child, and caring for her was relatively easy.

As battalion personnel were reassigned to other units; work and responsibilities fell on remaining staff members. To assure timely compliance to tasks, we followed a timeline synchronizing primary and secondary tasks. Staff update meetings were held with the commander at least three times a week. Separate meetings with regimental headquarters and the company commander and staff were held as needed.

Finally, one night I was told the missing lieutenant was in her quarters. Leaving the child with a neighbor, I drove on post to sit up with the lieutenant until she was safely transferred for professional care. Exhausted, I drove home, changed my clothes, and went to work. I had a lot to do. The transition staff was busy transferring property, reassigning personnel, maintaining equipment to transfer to gaining units, and practicing for the unit deactivation ceremony. My days were full, and I was fatigued from nights with little or no sleep.

The squadron commander had to sign the lieutenant's release from our squadron for reassignment to the hospital. He was a caring sensitive officer who hesitated to sign her release because it could have ended her career. He spoke with her doctor before signing. I hated to release her too, but I was convinced the lieutenant should not be in the Army and that we had to keep her safe and help her to become well. One of the lieutenant's sisters came to get her niece just before the start of the school year.

Before I knew it, deactivation day arrived. What an unbelievable two-plus months. I worked hard to get through my military requirements while creating safe environments for the lieutenant and her niece.

Nearly every organization on Fort Polk had representatives present at the Squadron deactivation ceremony. I was proud to be a woman ceremonial commander of troops and of combat support units. I heard I was the first woman. I was honored for the experience of being an executive officer of a combat support squadron, being their command of troops and having the privilege of reviewing them in a half-track, an armored vehicle mobile on two front wheels and tracked rear. This was a dream come true.

The ceremony was executed like clockwork.

The regimental commander was pleased. My squadron commander was happy, stating he enjoyed working with me. He complimented my work and added, "You are very talented. I have not worked with anyone better than you. I wish you had served with me earlier in my command."

His words meant more than he knew because I knew I could do the job; I just needed an opportunity.

Officers and soldiers from across the post were shaking my hand, offering congratulations.

One lieutenant from the engineer company said, "Ma'am, this is one of the proudest days of my career. I was so glad to know you." That stuck with me.

I responded, "I understand lieutenant, it is one of my proudest days also."

The weather was hot and humid, like only Louisiana summers can be. Yet again I had burned through a barrier. Sweat poured down my face hiding my tears of pride. All my work was manifested in that moment. Exhausted, I stood to serve another day, but my time in this regiment was over. True to his word, the regimental commander assisted in my transfer to a logistics position on a brigade staff located across post.

CHAPTER 18

FIND SOMETHING WRONG

———

"Attention to orders …" the brigade adjutant reads.

I was promoted to the rank of major in a small ceremony in the brigade conference room. I have lots of guests from the church, my assignment in the regiment, and home. My mother, sister, and my sister's mother-in-law—my good friend—traveled from North Carolina to Fort Polk, Louisiana to witness my transition from company to field-grade officer.

After a year of stress-free duty as the brigade logistics officer, I took the support operations officer in a logistics battalion just as the brigade was getting a new commander.

The new brigade commander was literally a ranger in special forces. We were told he was sent to our brigade while he was recovering from an illness. My move to the logistics battalion gave me the opportunity to branch qualify in the rank of major; I wanted the executive officer position.

The battalion commander was a nice guy, a West Point graduate, but very awkward. The battalion was not in the best state of readiness which rightfully didn't sit well with the brigade commander. He was also a West Point graduate. He pressured us to bring the unit up to standard.

On our first brigade run, the commander ran over five miles at a pace scattering people over the entire run. I thought the ragged formation looked ridiculous, but I guess he had something to prove. I didn't drop out. I could see him looking at me out of the corner of his eye, so I kept running. I think he was testing my endurance, and I wanted to show I was up to the task.

I didn't have much contact with him, but from a distance I thought he was dynamic, had a strong command presence, was fit, and knew the Army—just a great leader. I attended an event where he was the keynote speaker, and he was excellent. I liked him in many ways.

My battalion was tasked to provide support to a special forces unit that was scheduled to train at the Joint Readiness Training Center here at Fort Polk. Support Operations was my responsibility, and I was happy to have the work. I believed the training would be a treat for my staff.

Months before the special forces unit arrived, I researched their capabilities to project every possible mission they might need us to support. I attended every preparatory meeting to build the relationships needed to assure quick reaction logistics in support of our customers in every contingency.

My brigade commander and his point of contact at Fort Bragg agreed to limit the scope of the exercise to what was briefed in the operations briefs and concepts of operations. This was great because logistically the scope set the perimeters for our customer requirements during the exercise. I would stage what I knew the customer had requested ahead of the time, and I would forecast future needs based on their estimated rate of usage—nothing to it.

During the planning period leading to the exercise, I wrote and modified our plan of support for the operation and my staff, and I briefed and trained the company leaders whose soldiers would execute the plan.

When the exercise started, I believed the battalion support operations and the logistics units in the battalion were trained and ready. I also believed I could not make a mistake and that logistics could not be the cause of mission delay nor mission failure. We were ready!

Logistics evacuators from the corps at Fort Bragg arrived to observe, rate, and evaluate our support operations. My senior evaluator was a distant acquaintance from my first assignment in Korea; we both attended the Gospel Church service. We chatted as he followed me every step of the way. Seeing him was good, and he seemed happy to see me, too.

When the first special forces unit arrived at Alexandria airport, my battalion moved to the field. Our first support mission was to transport the soldiers to their marshalling area.

On the first day, I briefed an omnibus support plan that explained the interoperability and synchronization of units. In the evening out briefing, all support missions were run successfully.

Support operations were awesome on the second day. Every contingency was forecasted, and there were no deficiencies. My evaluator combed through my standard operating procedures to check the level of knowledge from battalion to individual soldier levels. The soldiers knew our operating procedures; there were no deficiencies found. I was proud of the soldiers; they knew the plan and were executing it flawlessly.

That evening my evaluator became inexplicably hostile toward me. He ignored me and talked to my noncommissioned officers instead. I didn't understand what caused his change. The friendly expression on his face when he arrived had become unwelcoming and maybe even frustrated.

He didn't speak to me at all the morning of the third day. Everyday all logistics requirements were completed according to plan. My noncommissioned officers started pushing me to complain because the logistics operations and soldiers were not receiving commendable ratings for their work.

On the last day of the exercise my Brigade changed the wargame to exceed the agreed upon scope. And that notionally placed the resupply points locations that exceeded our organic logistics support capabilities. The terrain didn't support ground transportation, so I requested air assistance, but aerial transportation was not included in the wargame scenario. At the evening meeting, the evaluator briefed the deficiency without explaining air support was not available.

The next day the exercise ended. At the out briefing, the impossible supply delivery was marked as the support operation's only deficiency. My staff was upset. I ignored the deficiency and made commendations for the soldiers through our battalion.

My evaluator didn't say anything to me at the end of the exercise, and I was a little disappointed because we were old friends just five days ago.

A year later while walking across campus at Command and General Staff College, Fort Leavenworth, Kansas, I recognized the major who evaluated me at Fort Polk as he passed me on the sidewalk. He recognized me, too, and said hello. It was like old times. He paused, "I want to apologize to you for the way I acted at Fort Polk. I know you probably hate me, but I was ordered to find something wrong with your work. I am very sorry for the way everything happened."

I let what he said roll over in my mind. He had to find something wrong; well that makes since to me.

I responded, "That is all right, man. I don't hate you. I was confused by the way you acted, but I am not surprised by what you are saying now. I knew something had happened when your personality changed. I was disappointed, but believe me, I have had worst days."

He continued, "But you don't understand … It was not alright. My checklist was approved before leaving Fort Bragg. My job should have been easy because your guys were completing every task without any deficiencies, not even for area cleanliness.

"Yes, we trained hard to educate everybody and synchronize our efforts with our customer's needs."

"Cleola, your brigade commander said there had to be something wrong with your operation. He told my boss to find some deficiencies in your area because every other section had deficiencies. And I was told not to give your section any commendations."

As I listened, I was not surprised. This kind of underhandedness had become so routine.

He continued, "My supervisor told me, either I find something wrong, or he will find someone who will. I didn't know what to do, so I began looking deep to find something. I feel bad about it. I tried to be neutral, but I was told that you weren't perfect—no one is perfect."

"Well major, they were right; no one is perfect, but our planning for the conditions of that exercise were as perfect as we could make it. I wish you had told me what was going on; I would have helped you find a fault acceptable for them without disappointing the soldiers. My noncommissioned officers were upset because they knew some of the soldiers deserved commendable ratings."

He looked up from the ground, "Really? You would have found a fault."

"Yes, we could have worked something out together, and my soldiers would have supported you, too. I didn't care about the evaluation. There are many things that we could have done better, you know … as they said, no one is perfect. I am sorry you were pressured because of me. The stress and worry weren't worth it."

"Well, Cleola, I am sorry the soldiers didn't get what they deserved and your noncommissioned officers …"

Laughing, "They really had strong words for you, Sir—no love for you at all."

He said, "I didn't know what to do. So, I was glad you didn't complain about me, and I am glad to see you now—to have this chance to let you know what happened."

I answered, "I am glad, too. I am not surprised by anything in the Army anymore, and at least now, we can be friends again."

As we talked, I started to feel bad for him. He is a man trying to provide for his family; he was hurt by the experience because he had feelings. I was glad he got to clear his conscience.

We talked a little longer, remembering the fun days at church in Korea. He remembered me as a soloist, and it was true; I enjoyed singing.

Together we exclaimed, "That church was on fire!" We laughed.

Then we paused. The pressure was off, and we were okay with each other. We hugged as friends and bid each other farewell before walking away in different directions.

CHAPTER 19

BELOW ZONE

At the halfway point of my tour in Korea, a battalion executive officer position was opening in DISCOM. To take the position I would need to extend my stay in Korea six additional months. The DISCOM commander, Colonel Heston, was the approving authority for the job, so I asked for an office call with him to make him aware of my interest in the position. I reminded him that I was the only command and general staff college graduate who was not placed in the branch qualifying position promised to all graduates. Instead, I was placed in a relatively minor staff job with his assurance that the next executive officer position would be mine. He recalled his promise to place me in the next opening position, so we talked pleasantly about my outstanding qualifications and my performance in my current position.

A few days passed before the DISCOM executive officer, Lieutenant Colonel Jefferson, called me to her officer. She was Black. After committing me to secrecy, she shared the commander was working to bring one of the officers he mentors to take the battalion executive officer position. While working in her office one night, she overheard a phone conversation between the two men coordinating the move. She agreed with me that what he was doing wasn't right but said she couldn't get involved because the DISCOM commander was her rater. She handed me a copy of the incoming major's officer record brief.

I read: Major Pixley, Caucasian male, entered the Army a year ahead of me, works in assignments at Army Personnel Command. Reading more I discovered he was already branch qualified and he had already held the position of battalion executive officer. I lowered the page, breathe then read it again. This was dishonest, demoralizing, and discriminatory; I was tired of it. Pixley was receiving an undeserved advantage at my expense. I had not been rated in a battalion executive officer position, and the DISCOM commander was saving it for a man who had had the position—why? Also, Major Pixley would be moving at government expense to Korea from Washington, DC to take the job he would hold for a second time.

Jefferson said, "That major would not be coming here from Washington, DC without the approval of his chain of command at Personnel Command. The DISCOM commander couldn't move Pixley without help. He was someone's boy."

I knew she was right. Major Pixley worked under the two-star general who headed the Logistics Personnel Management Branch. Someone in that office signed his orders.

I waited a few days to give Colonel Heston the opportunity to let me know someone else was selected for the position. He didn't say anything, so after command and staff meeting, I asked to talk with him.

In our meeting he said, "I know what you want to know, and I have selected a great officer to take the upcoming battalion executive officer position. I know that we talked about it, but it is too late now. I have already promised an officer the job, and he is preparing to come."

His statement was so matter of fact it catches me off guard.

He continued, "I selected him because he needs the position to make him competitive for selection to lieutenant colonel, below zone."

I was astonished, "Thanks for your honesty, but, well Sir, following the guidance in Army regulation 600-8-29, I will be competitive for promotion below zone, also. I have been told many times that I am exceptional and talented. Why not help me? The executive officer position is probably all that I need. I have the qualifications to fill that position, and I am here, in division and in this country, which saves the Army transportation costs."

He said, "Well, yes, you are good, but he is already on his way and there is nothing I can do about it."

I walked from his office next door to Lieutenant Colonel Jefferson, "Ma'am, this is not right. I need your help. I am tired of being oppressed, abused, and run over by racist, White males. You know Colonel Heston is discriminating against me. He admitted Major Pixley is getting the job so he can be selected below zone, ahead of his peers. The regulation was not intended to be manipulated in this way. Below zone officers selected must be truly outstanding and clearly superior to those who would otherwise be selected from in or above the promotion zone. What was happening is disparate treatment and Colonel Heston was not trying to hide his intent to the discriminate. He was just moving this guy over me because he wants him to succeed. They do this stuff all the time."

She said, "Good ole boy."

"Yes, good ole boy or mentoring. When I entered the Army, mentoring was part of leadership. Now, mentoring was a buzzword used by 'leadership' to loosely discriminate for, and cheat for, the people they want to succeed. Heston is in a leadership position over us, but he is not our mentor. He doesn't provide us guidance; he doesn't teach us anything. He barely speaks to us, and now he is overtly discriminating against me without fear of penalty."

The Lieutenant Colonel Jefferson said, "I know Cleo, but I can't do anything about it. I warned you this was going to happen to stop you from extending your time in Korea with hopes for a job you can't get. It's not right but what can I do? This is how things are."

"I understand that you want to protect your career, Colonel Jefferson, but what good is it to make it to top if you are too scared to speak against what is wrong? Help me stop this, not just for me but for the Black women who will follow us."

She didn't help, so I asked the deputy division commander for help, but he really couldn't do anything either. Since he was an infantryman, he couldn't override command authority within logistics branches.

I knew it was a long shot, but I sent a letter of complaint to the Department of the Army but never got a response from them. After all, I was probably writing to guys who also cheated the system to get where they were.

Within two months, the major arrived and took the position. I treated him as a professional. We were civil to each other.

I only had sixty days left in Korea. My sergeant major—Sergeant Major White, who witnessed the happenings during our tour—and I were talking. "Ma'am, I have never seen an officer treated like you. I always thought the best officers got promoted and placed in command. I have seen how hard you work and how smart you are. You are the best officer

I have ever worked with, and I spent most of my life in the Airborne at Fort Bragg."

I responded, "Thanks sergeant major, I appreciate your support, but this is the way it has always been for me. I'm tired of them, and I don't have to take this because I have a good life outside this racist Army."

The sergeant major leaned forward, "That man, Colonel Heston, is the worst. He shouldn't get away with this. You are a true professional, Ma'am, and you know more than them. That's why they treat you this way … they are jealous."

I replied, "I don't care what they think of me, sergeant major, because they couldn't think less of me than I think of them."

I paused.

"Sergeant major, I will not walk into a job, salute Major Pixley, and call him Sir! No way! I will never respect him. He knows that he is cheating to move ahead. I don't see how he can respect himself."

"You know Ma'am, who knows how many of them—people like Heston and Pixley—got their positions through this process?"

"Sergeant major, I believe most do. From what I have seen, officers must have a mentor or someone to protect you before selection to battalion command. Our military record is secondary or tertiary to an officer's advancement. If this is true, that would explain much of what happened so many times during my career. A general officer once told me that my combat service wouldn't count towards my career progression."

"Ma'am, you are right, I would never have believed this happened in the Army if I wasn't seeing it for myself. Combat service is what counts! I thought the officers I worked with were in their positions because they were the best … until I met Heston. He is sitting in a job, not knowing anything. He depends on you to do his work. You write him a script, so he can brief his concept of support plan to the general. He is pitiful. I have seen staff officers make bullet slides and give their officer briefing cards but … a full script, even telling him when to pause," sergeant major chuckled, "that is too much. How did he become a DISCOM commander?"

"I guess the system set him up for success, too, sergeant major. Like this guy, Major Pixley, was managing the records of his peers. In that position, I guess he realized his record wasn't good enough to place him ahead of his peers, so he and his mentors are doctoring the situation to make him appear superior. Disgusting! The system is such a mess, so full of White male liars and cheaters. I believe they think the right is theirs to do what is necessary to maintain control over the Army."

Sergeant major said, "They have their right, but you have your rights, too. The question is, where do their rights end and yours begin? You have as much right as Pixley to have the job."

I answered, "In my opinion they think their rights never end. Their rights extend beyond the constitution to a place of White male supremacy. The constitution gives rights to all Americans. It does not say that White men have to be in the majority and in charge. As long as an American is in charge, constitutional perimeters are met. If Black women head the entire logistics of the Army, it would still be the United States Logistics Corps. I believe they are afraid that if they don't cheat, they will not maintain the majority. Neither Heston nor Pixley would ever be able to beat me, honestly. Sergeant major, if I get to the top, things will surely change; everyone will have an equal opportunity."

"You bet Major Davis. Do you think Heston and that battalion commander will give Pixley a fair performance evaluation? He is entering that job knowing he can't fail."

"Yeah sergeant major. He is all but assured a top-rated officer evaluation report and his career will be accelerated because he will be selected to the rank of lieutenant colonel a year ahead of his peers.

Sergeant Major White shook his head, "Um, um, um, it is not good for soldiers to have commanders like them. Look at Heston, he doesn't know anything. I've worked with I don't know how many officers as jumpmaster in the Airborne, you stand right there with the best of them."

My mind wandered and so did the focus of our conversation, "You know sergeant major, I followed a captain in command who became my assignment officer; on its face you know that shouldn't happen but anyway the system allows it. While I was deployed commanding in combat, he was in D.C. enjoying family and all that comes with it. The next year, he was selected below zone to major and this year he was selected below zone to lieutenant colonel. He is two years ahead of me and the other officers who started in our year group.

"Two years ahead, Ma'am?

"Two years, sergeant major! The mission of the US military is to fight the country's wars. That is a fact. So, what could that captain have done to merit his selection to higher rank before those in his year group that went to war? What could he have done to make him better qualified than his peers who are veterans? Even if he has met all training requirements and has four doctoral credentials, that does not lift him to level equal to combat veteran. What made him clearly superior to those who would otherwise be selected?"

Sergeant major interrupted. "They have rank but they know nothing, like Colonel Heston."

"Yes, you are right I wouldn't do what they are doing because I want to be the best. I only want a system that is just. Justice and equal opportunity are not too much to expect from the Army especially since they are constitutional guarantees. I am as much a citizen as anyone born in the United States. The Army is not a private commercial entity, it is owned, 'in common' by the American people. I have the right to excel according to my merits.

Sergeant major responded, "Now Ma'am, they are not going to put that in a regulation because if they, did people like you who work hard trying to get promoted wouldn't have a reason to join the Army. The Army wouldn't have any officers."

I thought for a few minutes, "It is disgusting to see White officers both cheat and claim intellectual superiority at the same time. Like a game of leapfrog, they pull each other up and over to positions of leadership based solely on race. They don't care about the emotional and psychological effect of their racism; it is about maintaining power and control. They have no shame; they are Machiavellian. The end justifies the means, and the end will always be White male dominance. They don't have to hide their racism because their privilege and authority is unchecked, deeply layered in rule changes to cheat and so entrenched in unwritten traditions that only crushing and rebuilding the system at its foundation will fix it."

My sergeant major took a breath, "I have never seen anything like this; these are the worst officers I have ever seen, or maybe I should say the worst officers I have ever known about."

Reflecting, "Sergeant major, I appreciated Colonel Heston's honesty. I have some comfort knowing I didn't do anything to deserve his mistreatment and that Pixley had done nothing to deserve preference. The officers at Personnel Command and this DISCOM commander are really to blame for Pixley. Some of the senior officers are the problem; they have the power to abuse the system, and they exploit that power with random abuse. They should not have their hands in positioning officers, but they do sometimes interfere when officers are in the ranks of lieutenant and captain. Back in the day we called them 'good ole boys'; today this is called mentoring. The system is corrupt because they are personally manipulating a system that by design is meant to run on competition and excellence. Their interference creates and perpetuates the environment of discrimination, abuse, and hostility directed towards people like me."

A few months later, I received a top block evaluation report and orders to a normative position in Hawaii! Who could complain about that assignment?

My military tour in Korea was over. As I packed the car to leave, wonderful memories of my first tour here flowed through my mind. I was so young, innocent, and excited when I arrived over twelve years ago. There in the distance, the source of pride for maintenance officers, the 702 Maintenance Battalion open-ended wrench, still high on the mountain with the words "Raise Up Maintenance" emblazoned defiantly for all to see. The officer's club where my friends and I had meals, partied, and had so much fun stood in the corner empty and unused. As Sergeant Major White and I rode down the street, I saw soldiers running in formation, a battalion practicing on the parade field, and new recruits in-processing through the division reception station called the "Turtle Farm."

Up the hill to our left was the DISCOM Chapel—a sanctuary for the abused, oppressed, and overlooked—where

God made over and restored them with strength to endure the hateful world. Across the street was the Gateway Club, an all-ranks club that had the best American meals north of Seoul. I smiled as the full statue of the division's emblem, an indigenous American Chef dressed in full battle feathers and regalia, appeared standing in the center of the traffic circle. He was the symbol of strength and pride in this division. He was a *warrior!* I really enjoyed my time in service, and I loved the Army. I mean really loved it—the way a battered wife loves and cleaves to an abusive husband. I loved all the soldiers and noncommissioned officers who made me excel and appear invincible. I loved leading and problem solving, ruck matching and fitness training, training in the field and traveling to foreign lands. I loved soldiering and being a soldier. I was thankful to all the officers who stood for what was right when the choice was there for them to turn on me and leave me hanging. I thanked God for putting the Army in perspective: It was a job. It didn't define me; it was just a job. I was so much bigger than anything man could do to me, and no matter what the challenge, I would not be defeated!

As the sergeant major and I rolled out of the Camp Casey security gate, I saluted the military policemen standing on guard. Sergeant major stopped at the traffic signal just out of the gate.

"This is it, sergeant major," I said. "I am out of the Army. I've had enough. I am done."

Sergeant major responded, "Me too ma'am, I am out, too. I am turning down a command sergeant major position; my next assignment will be my last one. I need to spend time with my wife and two boys, and after seeing what happened to you here, I have had enough. If I had not seen it for myself,

I would not have believed it. Just remember I will always be here for you."

I shook my head in acknowledgement.

The light changed. Sergeant major turned left toward Seoul and accelerated; I did not look back.

CHAPTER 20

ALOHA MEANS GOOD-BYE

My assignment to Pacific Command Headquarters, Camp Smith, Honolulu, Hawaii, was to placate me for the injustice at Camp Casey. I was satisfied because I was in a joint assignment; all defense service branches worked together, but by coincidence my senior Army officer—a one star general—was a major at my first assignment in Korea when I was a lieutenant. What a coincidence, indeed. I knew how the White officer network work. They stayed in contact with each other, and I believe they made decisions of promotions and advancements outside official channels.

Other than nightmares of my past, my joint assignment was awesome! This was the perfect place of peace to end my career. Everyone in the office liked me; I liked all of them. We worked well together and socialized together after duty hours and on weekends.

The office environment was as beautiful as the weather outside. My work section was a mixture of Air Force, Naval officers, some civilians, and me—a real joint force office.

Our officer in charge—a Navy captain—was calm, "laid back," cordial, and so was everyone in the office. A Navy captain is equivalent to an Army colonel in rank, which is the rank of a DISCOM commander. For the first time in my career, I felt appreciated for just doing my job. This is how my career should have been; this must be how it felt to just be an officer.

I didn't expect to make lieutenant colonel, but my name was on the list. Other than for purposes of retirement pay, I didn't care. I didn't want the usual fake ceremony grinning and fronting as my senior officer pinned on my rank. So, I flew to Washington, DC—to the Pentagon—where several friends were stationed, to have Colonel (retired) Everett Mickelson speak at my pinning. Colonel Mickelson was the division operations officer who spoke up to save my company command and career in Saudi Arabia when I was attending my father's funeral in the United States.

The ceremony was small. My mother was there to pin me, and my sister, Sarah, was there supporting me as always. During my speech, I announced this would be my last promotion because I was getting out of the Army. I mentioned it to make it final! But that day and evening we celebrated with good food, music, and loving company.

I returned to Hawaii a lieutenant colonel focused on transitioning to the civilian life. Some of my fellow officers tried to convince me to stay in the Army and fight. Fight—not me, I'd been fighting all along; the system was institutionally biased in favor of White men, and I had had enough. I would not walk into an office and salute a man I knew was ethically, technically, and professionally beneath me. The system was corrupt and replicated itself through its leadership. I would not waste more time hoping to fix it.

Actually, my career ended years ago when I came out of the desert. Since that time, I had not been the same, as if I lost my innocence. I saw the ugliness under its veneer; I have not felt the same about the Army.

Each year, hundreds of young Black women are commissioned into the Army as innocent and eager as I was when I joined. What can I say to any one of them if asked how to succeed in the Army? "Get to know a general and ride his coat tails" is not an acceptable answer, but it is the answer. Before company command you will need an individualized "mentor" to guide your career forward. Oh, yes, and remember to smile, stay focused on your success, and protect your interest.

What good is it to be a leader who is afraid to protect all your subordinates? Having a select group of officers gliding to success along the top while the masses are entrenched in the working underclass with limited opportunities of advance is a form of servitude.

My final move was to North Carolina, to be near my mother, and I could revert to the lady I was raised to be. I sang and played gospel music as I drove to out process the Army at Fort Jackson, South Carolina, March 31, 2003. I cried the entire ninety-minute drive there. The day was beautiful. The sun was shining just over the trees that were still naked from winter. Of course, some memories haunted life like a friendly ghost. I had had an awesome career, so many soldiers to thank, and the noncommissioned officers who I owe so much. Especially the noncommissioned officers in my company and my first sergeant. They carried me through the lowest point of my life. And Sergeant Major White who was with me when I decided to end my military service. I wondered if any of my officers would become senior officers. I hope they did well because they deserved to do well.

I have seen some beautiful places. The beautiful richness of the people of Saudi Arabia was breathtaking. And the crowded Korean markets, their folks dancing, singing, and drumming—awe-inspiring. In Texas, I went to the rodeo and ate nachos for the first time; and I ate gumbo, po' boys, and beignets in Louisiana. Those are sights and sounds that last a lifetime. I am thankful.

I wiped my face before entering the gate at Fort Jackson. Leaving the Army was a big step for some but not for me; I was so ready. This was one of the happiest days of my life, and I praised God. I entered the Army passionate and motivated, intending to excel. I was naive and ill prepared for the mendacity, hatred, and misogyny that persist throughout my career. My ability to mentally survive the abuse and do my job was miraculous. I was thankful.

Now, I had done my journey. The clerk handed me my retirement form.

Pointing she said, "Read it to make sure the information is complete and correct, then sign here."

My heart was thumping as I read each line. I signed my name. She looked at it and handed me the original.

I asked," Is that it?"

The clerk answered, "Yes, Ma'am, that is it."

Walking to my car, I took a deep breath filled my lungs with air, and burst into tears of joy.

"Thank you, God! Thank you, God! I made it."

CHAPTER 21

FIX IT

——

"So, Mr. Jones, that is how it happened. I left the Army to free myself from the burdensome suffocating weight of injustice. I guess that is why seeing a man murdered on television triggered memories of my career."

"What they did was certainly wrong, Ms. Davis."

"Yes, what was done to you was wrong and unnecessary too, Mr. Jones. You were an awesome second lieutenant, one to be celebrated by all Americans. They could have given you both the same medal. Please accept my sincere apology. I am sorry that you were denied the honor you deserve, which is the Silver Star medal." (Army Regulation: AR 600-8-22)

"I led that platoon for seven months through the Tet Offensive in January 1968. During my time as the leader, we killed, captured, and destroyed more enemy soldiers, weapons, and food supplies than any other like-sized unit in the First Brigade." (Duff, 2017)

"That was amazing; you and your soldiers were amazing."

"Though I was wounded in action in another mission, and had soldiers suffer wounds, I never had a soldier killed under my leadership. *To God be the glory!*"

"Yes, to God be the glory for the things he has done."

"Well, Ms. Davis, I have learned a lot about you. You should be proud of the service you gave to your country and of yourself for persevering many challenges along the way."

"Thank you for listening, Mr. Jones. Every time I tell my story I heal a bit more. I probably could have put it behind me, but like it is with your medal, the issues that followed me from service remain unresolved. Army has a racial problem, and the leaders of this government are doing little to fix the situation. I am surprised at the number of Black officers who share experiences like mine but are reluctant to call their mistreatment racist. I believe that it is our responsibility to bring our disparate separate treatment to the forefront because we are the affected parties. The system needs our input to create the transparency that will prevent another generation of Black officers from fighting racial discrimination and White supremacy."

I pause to open my computer. "When you have time Mr. Jones, I sent you an article from *USA Today* that provides haunting revelations of racism, "The lack of Black officers in the Army's combat commands has diminished the chances for diversity in military leadership for years to come, resulting in a nearly all-white leadership of an increasingly diverse military and nation. The Army, the largest of the armed services, has made little progress in promoting officers of color, particularly Black soldiers, to commands in the past six years."" (Thomas, 2020)

"Yes, I think I've read this one, Ms. Davis, and so many others like it. One search on my computer provides articles that go back ten to fifteen years addressing the shortages of Black officers in Army command and leadership positions."

"Oh, my goodness, Mr. Jones, Californian Representative Jackie Speier didn't mince words when calling the lack of diversity in the Army a 'glaring example of structural racism … Failure to cultivate leadership that is truly representative of America threatens troop morale and cohesion … The strength and future of our armed forces is its diversity. Congress has a duty to ensure military leadership understand and heed that fact.'(Thomas,2020) I pray that she is serious, and something is done to fix things."

"Me too, but do you think it will take congressional intervention to fix it? The Army can fix it."

"We are only two examples of what is probably hundreds more. The data and discussion in this article reflect what happens when an authoritarian institution like the Army is absent of checks and punitive devices. The system is corrupt, and in the words of the congresswoman, racist. (Thomas,2020) If congress is the solution, I welcome it."

I remember hearing that a senator got involved in sexual harassment legislations; maybe Congress should be involved.

"The absence of leadership is the problem, Mr. Jones. When I joined the Army, mentoring was an intricate part of leadership. My battalion commander held officer training meetings for his officers, and he made it clear that the training and guidance (the definition of mentoring) of his lieutenants was part of his job. I wonder what happened to that kind of leader. Back then officers mentored their subordinates; that way developing officers received mentoring from numerous leaders as they matured in their profession.

Four years later, at the rank of captain, I became aware a personalized mentorship system existed when some of my peers were 'mentored' into command before others of us. At the end of my career, mentoring had replaced leadership. An assignment meant following the orders of my senior officer in a hostile environment devoid of integrity, leadership, and mentorship."

"You have seen some tough situations, Ms. Davis."

"Yep, but the manipulation of systems to assure the selection of one major below zone was too much. It brings to question both the need for below-zone selections and implies dishonestly in officer evaluation reporting. Do you think the selected major's performance will receive scrutiny by the colonel who brought him into the job? Officer evaluation reporting is subjective to the point of being freelance. I'm sure the major got an outstanding performance evaluation. And the award system that affords the rescued officer to receive a more prestigious award than you, the officers who gallantly saved him while under fire—it makes me sick Mr. Jones."

"I hear you and understand what you are saying, Ms. Davis; a lot needs to be done. Excuse me a second. I have family coming in the house. It has been a long day. Thanks for sharing your story and listening to my story, as well. We will talk again soon."

"Yes, Thank you Mr. Jones. I know you have to go, and so do I. God Bless you."

"Good-bye. Ms. Davis, God Bless you, too."

"Good-Bye, Mr. Jones."

ACKNOWLEDGEMENTS

Forged in Battle supporters and contributors, please accept my sincere thanks for your support and the words of encouragement. You inspired me to push hard when faced with the challenges that come with becoming an author. I cannot express how much the making of this book means to me. The most rewarding and the most distressing parts of my life meet here to fulfill my dream. I couldn't have made it without you.

To my proofreaders and fact checkers, thank you for your confidence in me, your time, and your kind thoughts.

Special thanks to my friend, retired Colonel James Jones. Your story is what inspires movies and monuments. I appreciate your leadership, patience, and guidance. I am honored to know you and to call you friend. Blessings to you and your family.

And

Special Thanks to my friend, Nickey, who invited me to join the program that literally walked me through the creative writing process needed to write *Forged in Battle*.

Finally, thanks to my family … my cousins who have shown so much love and support, but especially my sister Sarah who has always encouraged me to write my story. I love you all.

To all who helped, please accept my gratitude.

APPENDIX

CHAPTER 2

- Powers, Rod. "How the U.S. Army Is Organized." The Balance Careers. Updated on April 26, 2019. https://www.thebalance-careers.com/u-s-army-military-organization-from-squad-to-corps-4053660.

CHAPTER 15

- Ferraro, Thomas. "Desert Storm Celebration." UPI Archives. June 9, 1991. www.upi.com/archives/1991/06/09/ Desert-Storm-Victory-Celebration.

CHAPTER 21

- Brook, Tom Vanden. "Where Are the Black Officers? US Army Shows Diversity in Its Ranks but Few Promotions to the Top." USA Today. Updated September 1, 2020. https://www.usatoday.com/in-depth/news/politics/2020/09/01/military-diversity-army-shows-few-black-officers-top-leadership/3377371001/.

- Duff, Carol. "The Tet Offensive and Its Aftermath." *Veterans Today*. December 2, 2017. https://www.veteranstoday.com/2017/12/02/the-tet-offensive-and-its-aftermath/.